POACHERS, CRANBERRIES & SNOWSHOES

POACHERS, CRANBERRIES & SNOWSHOES

To Kasandra
From
C Shipley
15/6/04

Chuck Shipley
J.B.S. Publishing
2003

Cover design: Kevin Franco Designs

National Library of Canada Cataloguing in Publication Data

Shipley, Chuck, 1939-
   Poachers, cranberries & snowshoes / Chuck Shipley.

ISBN 0-9733461-0-8

   1. Shipley, Chuck, 1939- 2. Game wardens--Alberta--Anecdotes.
3. Outdoor
life--Alberta--Anecdotes. I. Title. II. Title: Poachers, cranberries
and snowshoes.
GV191.52.S54A3 2003   796.5'092   C2003-911051-6

Printed in Canada by Blitzprint Inc.

ACKNOWLEDGEMENTS.

If you ever sit down and put your memories on paper, you soon find out those memories are not really yours, they belong to everyone involved along the way. This book would not have been possible without the wit and the wisdom of all the people I encountered. My thirty-two years in the Fish and Wildlife Division allowed me to work with a never-ending stream of fascinating people. Couple this with no day the same as any other and you have the recipe for this book- my recollection of some extraordinary events and incredible people. Supported and encouraged along the way by family, I dedicate these stories to them and to all the people who were part of my adventure.

Disclaimer: (on advise of legal council)

The stories and incidents contained in this book are true. The names of the individuals involved have been changed or omitted to protect their identities. There is no intent to malign or denigrate anyone in telling these stories.

TABLE OF CONTENTS.

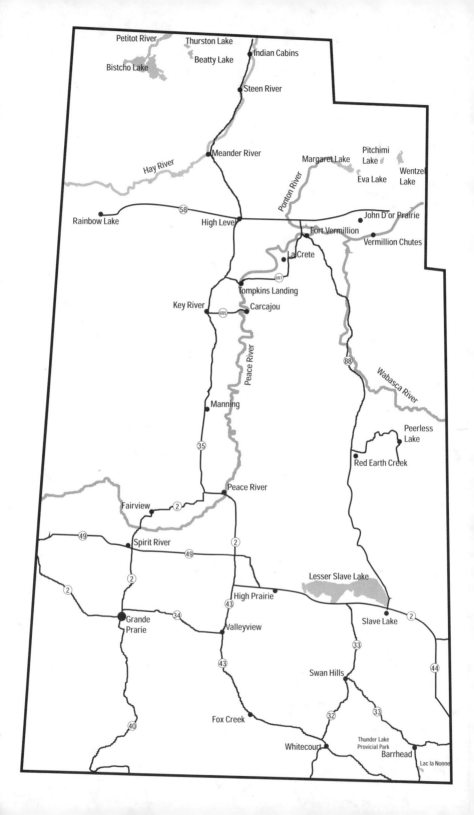

INTRODUCTION.

You know, if all this works out the way it is supposed to you will have before you a collection of stories about the life and times of an Alberta Fish and Wildlife Officer.....game warden, fish cop, "fish fuzz", "fins and feathers", the names tend to decline into the more and more unprintable. All the events took place from 1963 through to 1995, between Strathmore to the south and High Level in the north. Of course, where appropriate, names have been changed, if only to duck any ill-conceived lawsuits and to avoid any embarrassment to anyone, especially the author.

Strathmore was the beginning of an odyssey that lasted for the next thirty-two years. My career commenced on December 16, 1963, at the Strathmore Fish and Wildlife office. For me, the prospect of any new job has always been exciting; this one proved to be a real dandy! I was one of the lucky applicants chosen from around 400 for only 10 vacant positions. Not that I stayed in Strathmore long. May of 1964 saw my wife and I move north to Barrhead, the move occurring between stints of in-service training at the Forestry Training School in Hinton. Barrhead lasted until 1966 when I was transferred to High Level. Up north we went- myself, my wife, and one infant daughter. High Level was home until 1970, then it was off to High Prairie for five years, this time with a second infant daughter in tow. By the time we were posted to Edmonton for a further five years, our now not-so-infant daughters were not so sure about all this moving. 1980 saw one further posting to Rocky Mountain House, this time one that would see me through till buyout and retirement in 1995.

When you start a job like this, it always SOUNDS interesting, but I never had any idea the problems, the compromising situations, and the pure adrenalin rushes it would go on to produce over a span of thirty-two years. An airplane crash. A scalping and threatened suicide . Flipped truck. An aircraft chase. Bear attack. Belligerent hunters. Crazy poachers. The nuttiest of pranks. Not to mention the day to day shenanigans and escapades that are bound to occur when you are involved with animals and people. These stories represent a colorful world known to few that will get your attention.

Yes, my time in Strathmore was interesting enough, particularly in terms of meeting so many of the people who were actually doing the job I aspired to. All of them bar none had the most fascinating stories to tell, so much so I began to wonder if I would ever become involved in such incredible situations myself. It was all a far cry from writing my first ticket. That was for unattended trap lines, and I was more than just a little nervous. Not very exciting but it was a milestone, and a prelude to a great adventure.

The tales that follow are not necessarily in chronological order. Rather they are a collection of memories that I wanted to put on paper for my grandchildren, and for anybody else who might enjoy them. They recount actual events without any fancy footwork to "gussy them up".

So read and enjoy

THE AUTHOR

If you want an insight into the fascinating world of a Fish and Wildlife Officer in Alberta from the Sixties to the Nineties this book is for you. Chuck was no ordinary run of the mill game warden. Endowed, others might say cursed, with an outrageous sense of humor, his take on events was always unique, thoughtful and full of fun. This unique perspective on life is evident in this 30 story book.

Chuck and Jean are now living south of Rocky Mountain House in their retirement home. Chuck is presently serving his first term on the Clearwater County Council. Jean is retired and working part time at a local green house. Bonnie and Susan have gone on to successful carriers of their own.

Chuck continues to scribble the remainder of his memoirs in his spare time, anticipating another book.

1 ~ THE DEVIL MADE ME DO IT

Oh come on now, Christmas is a time for surprises. Some of them we like, some we don't. It's really a matter of perspective. I am of the mind if an opportunity arises, then one must entertain oneself, even though it may inconvenience others temporarily.

The insurance industry says it, the R.C.M.P. says it, anybody remotely associated with crime prevention says "Thou shalt not leave thy vehicle running unattended"...... even if it is fifty below outside and you zipped into the Post Office for your Christmas parcels. Thieves apparently hang around everywhere, especially the post office.

It was uncompromisingly winter in High Level, dark and very cold, about 4:30 in the afternoon, and a mere three days before Christmas day. I went off to the Post Office for the same reason I always go to the Post Office. It was a zoo. There were vehicles parked every which way around the building and spilling over into the vacant lot next door. People were bustling in and out with their Christmas mail, all intent on doing their business expeditiously and keeping warm. Almost every vehicle had been left running, unlocked and unoccupied. But there was one very special one, the local police cruiser. And there they were, two stalwart custodians of   The Law standing in the lineup, politely waiting their turn. Great!

Judging by the length of the line inside, I had lots of time. Quickly, I parked my truck at the very back of the lot, ran over to the cruiser, hopped in and backed it up, concealing it behind a very large transport truck, one of those eighteen wheel monsters. Yes, I took the keys; after all, I could not let just anybody steal it, could I? That would be too much of a story! I scurried back to my own truck, making sure that I had an unobstructed view of the front door of the Post Office so that I had a ringside seat for the coming action. As if to add to the tension, it was common knowledge that a police car had been stolen in Manning a few weeks earlier, and it was still missing. Manning was just down the road from us.

There they were, now at the front of the line, full of sweetness and light, collecting their mail. Shouldn't be too long now!

Out they came, exiting with a crowd of other people. It was so cold when an unexpected gust of wind blew a cloud of exhaust fumes around the group, they could not see their vehicles nor could I see them. When the cloud had dissipated, everyone but the two policemen had vanished. Truly, it was the Keystone Cops all over again. The uniformed men were rooted to the spot, their mouths agape in disbelief, their eyes wide in desperation, seeking out the car they knew should be there but somehow had gone AWOL.

I could see their mouths spewing a torrent of words, their heads turning frantically this way and that searching for their precious cruiser in the semi-darkness. No luck, no cruiser! This whole performance continued on for three or four minutes, suddenly coming to an abrupt halt. Both men were staring fixedly in my direction. Then they looked momentarily at each other, something was said, a decision was made, and they came marching towards me. Apparently, I had not hidden as well as I had thought. Their haste across the ice-covered parking lot saw what should have been a dignified stride degenerate into more of a semi-controlled sliding; either it was the ice or the thought I might know something about their car that generated such an unseemly haste. Finally they made it to my truck, so ever the good corporate citizen, I rolled down my window.

"Now what might you guys be up to?" I said cheerily.

The first and only words out of their mouths, and in unison no less, were the words "Where the Hell is our car?" Not "Excuse me sir, did you by chance see our police car?" or any other such polite enquiries, just "Where the Hell is our car?" I must be endowed with a mischievous countenance, otherwise I have no idea why they would have thought I knew anything about their car.

Bad luck struck again! The transport truck behind which I had hid their vehicle suddenly pulled out. There was the car in all its glory, and not ten yards away. They heard the truck and turned, spotted their cruiser and immediately made for it as if it was a long-lost friend.

"You might need these" I yelled, flinging the car keys in their direction. I left without looking back; it never pays to give a man in uniform a second chance- I should know!

There was, inevitably, an unfortunate consequence for me. The officer in charge of the detachment had been a good friend of mine for a long time. The car-hiding caper was one of those stories too good to keep to myself so I told him what happened, but only after he promised he would do nothing. Well, he sort of did nothing. The new directives regarding vehicle security were not vague nor discreet enough to deflect the suspicions of the two officers that I informed their supervisor, and we both enjoyed a good laugh at their expense.

2 ~ AROMATHERAPY!

Put skunks and fish into the same sentence and you are sure to get a recipe for amusement.

One fine day in June, we took a call from a local farmer informing us that, unfortunately, he had killed a skunk. This did not seem to be earth-shaking news to us, but he went on to say that he had discovered subsequently it was a female, and she had left behind the cutest litter of eight baby skunks. Not having the heart to kill them, he decided he would be smart and pass such an odorous problem to the Fish and Wildlife Division. No doubt, skunks are quite common, and they can even be cute; certainly they make wonderful pets if they are de-scented. Of course, at this particular juncture, there was no feasible way to have the procedure done on wild skunks and then to keep them as pets. Unhappily, the only avenue open was to destroy them.

By now it was close to suppertime. Prior to the phone call for help, my wife had suggested she would like to go for a drive.

"Why not combine business with pleasure?" she asked. "We could take a light supper and eat it at Thunder Lake after we have dealt with your skunk problem." Since she added she had never seen baby skunks before, I decided it was a great idea. Off we went in our station wagon.

There was the farmer waiting for us, but now it seemed the dog had tried to kill the skunks. To prevent the dog from getting bitten by an animal that often carries rabies, he had decided to kill them all himself. Since it was not a job I particularly relished, I thanked him.

"Would you mind getting rid of them for me?" he asked innocently.

Why not? He already had them in a burlap bag which I proceeded to put in the back of the station wagon. My wife was incredulous. Fish and Wildlife Officer though I was, did I not know that skunks had a propensity to stink to high heaven?

"Ah yes," I reassured her, "skunks can stink to high heaven, but not baby ones. They can't give off any odor because they have not yet developed their scent glands," I explained patiently. The boss had told me this so it had to be true. Guess again!

Not four hundred yards down the road, the station wagon, and by association its occupants, began to assume a very distinctive fragrance, a rather skunk-like aroma. Worse still, I had to be told this by an unimpressed wife because I have no sense of smell whatsoever. And I was told in very precise terms that left no room for interpretation. So now I was feeling some pressure to get them out of the car, which I did with some haste ,thankfully shutting the car door now that the problem was resolved. It was time to get back to enjoying our evening drive. That's when it was made clear to me, again in very precise language, the smell had not departed with the skunks, that, in fact, removing them made no difference at all. Now what? I decided the skunks were no reason why we could not go on to Thunder Lake for our picnic supper.

As are all new officers on a job, I was keen, I was enthusiastic, so when we got there, I took the opportunity to stop and check on some anglers even though I was informed, very clearly, I stank like a skunk. In order to reach the anglers, I had to walk by small knots of people standing around on the beach. I noticed that the first group stopped talking and studied me intently as I walked by. I thought nothing of that; after all, people always stare at other people in uniform. I had just made it past the next group when I heard a lady comment something to the effect that "something around here smells like skunk." Albeit somewhat grudgingly, I acknowledged to myself that it could be me but I carried on anyway to check out the anglers. Not one of them mentioned anything about a skunky smell so I began to question- Was it me that smelt like a skunk or was the lady just unimpressed with "fish fuzz" in general?

It was when I got back to the station wagon that it was reiterated, in no uncertain terms, I smelt like a skunk, and the smell had gotten worse.

"In fact, you reek," said my better half, emphasizing that home would be a very good place to go given the circumstances. I knew when to yield so away we went. On our arrival, we stripped off and hung all our clothes outside. Hot showers were in order, but alas the showers did not have the expected result. Oh for sure, we got ourselves clean, but much to my wife's chagrin, her long and luxurious black hair still emitted skunk. She re-showered alone. Again and again.

It was only the next day we found out the most successful way to remove the smell of skunks was to hang clothing up in a small room with an open bottle of formaldehyde. This neutralizes the scent of skunk very effectively we were told. Then all you have to do is to air out the clothes for a few minutes and you will get rid of the formaldehyde smell.

To this day we have avoided the distinctive smell of skunk in our marriage.

3 ~ YOU BE THE JUDGE

Out doing the patrol thing, somewhere between McLennan and High Prairie. It was a crisp winter day in November with one or two feet of snow. Everything was clinical white, the stuff of postcards of the Great White North. The fields were huge white blankets, clean and undisturbed.

Hold on a second, what was that? My truck slewed to a stop and out came the binoculars. Close to half a mile away, was a huge brown mound in the middle of all that snow. It didn't look right. As a matter of fact, it did not make sense, it looked too much like a moose. But then I could not see tracks of any kind near it, so what was the story? If it was a moose, surely it could not have died out there on its own, or could it? How did I get to it without leaving my own set of telltale tracks? After all, if it had been poached, I did not want to leave any sign that might persuade a poacher not to come back and pick up his trophy. Okay, so I'd just circle the general area in the truck and see if I could find any tire tracks leading over to the moose, if that was what it was.

Nothing to the west.

Nothing to the north.

Nothing to the east.

Last chance, to the south. Aha! Finally! Tire tracks going down a trail with bush and a deep ditch on both sides leading off in the direction of the moose. One set of tracks appeared to lead in, another set appeared to lead out. This called for a closer look. I headed down the trail and, within half a mile, there was an opening on the edge of the field. What do you think I could see from there? You guessed it! The brown hump in the snow that, at the first sighting might have been a moose transformed itself into reality: a very dead reality for the moose.

I was very careful not to get out of the truck where the other truck had stopped; there was no sense in leaving any sign that might tip off a returning poacher his game had been discovered. However, I could see quite clearly where someone had stood in what I presumed had been a rifleman's stance pointing in the direction of the moose. I checked around as best as I could from the inside of my truck to see if the poacher had left any brass, shell casings that could have been carelessly dropped, melting their way into the snow. No luck, if the moose had been shot, it had been shot from here. And there were no vehicle tracks from here to the moose. A further check with the binoculars revealed the animal's tracks right up to where it had fallen.

I made my way back to the main road from where I had first spotted the moose. It would have been a mighty long shot to knock a moose down in its tracks from here, but it could have been done. I made a point of going to the nearest house to ask if the occupants saw any hunters mooching around. I also hoped I would be able to discern whether they were lying when I asked if they had noticed the brown hump in the field. Not unexpectedly, the answers were "no" all round.

Now it was decision time. Should I go and have a close-up look at the dead animal and mark it for further identification? That would run the risk of my being discovered, but was it a risk worth taking? Or should I go and find somewhere to hide and see if anybody arrived to retrieve it? My curiosity got the better of me; I had to go and take a look. Since the people in the house knew what I was doing, what better place could there be than to start from the house? The grain field was a mile square with no fences; the moose was half to three quarters of a mile from the house. So be it. I drove through the foot and a half of snow right up to the carcass. I stopped my truck parallel to the back of the animal so I could get out and stand directly on the cadaver without leaving any footprints, the idea being that anybody driving up to the moose would not be spooked by human tracks. Clearly, the moose was shot very recently, so recently in fact the eyes did not have that typical glazed look of death, nor had it started to bloat. I got on to animal, took out my knife and carefully cut slits into both ears and carved my initials on the roof of its mouth. Then I hopped back into my truck and retraced my tracks out of the field. I certainly did not want anybody to see me near the moose.

From the road in front of the house, I went back to the start of the trail from which the moose had been shot. It so happened there was a T-intersection, the T being on its side. The long part of the T was the road I had just travelled. One end of the cross T pointed up the trail to the moose, the other end pointed down another main road. So where should I wait, the trickiest question of all? There were no trees around to conceal me, certainly none that were strategically located enough to allow me to view the moose and all access points to it without being seen myself. The tire tracks coming down the trail from the direction of the moose turned towards the main road where the house was located. This suggested to me that the hunter would come back the same way. I could only hope!

I decided to check out the road opposite the trail. It was the break I had been looking for; there was a gentle slope downward away from the trail to the moose, enough to provide the dead ground that would conceal most of my truck from all directions except the rear. It was not perfect but it would do the job, hopefully. I entered the details of my identifying the moose into my notebook in anticipation of a court case sometime in the future. This was in the days before we carried a camera as a regular part of our gear.

Darkness was settling in and I was as ready as I ever would be. My normal partner was currently on "days off" and since I couldn't find a neighboring officer, this whole deal would be solo. Was this to be one of those cases the old-time wardens used to talk about, where you had to wait and wait, and wait some more, and nobody ever shows up so you get mad , retrieve the moose, and call it a day? The only small consolation in that scenario was you got the moose that somebody else wanted.

An hour and something passed. There was no moon but the stars did provide a pallid light reflecting off the snow. Early on, the odd car trundled by on the main road about a mile away. Later there was nothing, just me, the snow, and the starlight; not even a coyote ventured out that night. The only sound to interrupt an otherwise bleak night was the country and western music I picked up from the local station on my truck's radio, and my engine idling quietly so I could keep warm.

Now what the hell was going on? That set of headlights I had just seen go by on the house on the main road should have reappeared down the road, but they did not. Okay then, I should turn off my motor. No wait, it would be better to back up a bit first because, where I was sitting, the hill in front would not hide the whole truck. I backed up, door open, leaning out, trying to keep out of their view. Feeling a lot more comfortable, I turned the truck off. Even though I was still hanging out the door, I could not hear a damn thing. There were no lights anywhere, what the hell was going on? Then came that adrenalin rush......!

Straight ahead where the trail to the moose began, lights. Both headlights and hand-held hunting lights pierced the night, panning through the darkness in every direction. I ducked instinctively but the hill screened me well. Yes, they now turned up the trail; thankfully it was so crooked and rough it claimed all of their concentration. Because of the deep ditches on both sides, they had enough on their plate without having to think about law enforcement.

Okay, decision time! Did I wait until they loaded their moose and were on their way back? Maybe they would head out a different way. Their truck looked very much like a 4X4 to me so they could head out in any direction they pleased. Finally I could not stand it any more, I had to go see what they were doing. If I was to start my truck while they were still moving, they would not hear me. So there we were, my truck now running with its lights off, their truck inching along ahead, lights now off also. My only hope was to trap them on the trail between the ditches. There was little danger that they would switch off their vehicle and hear me, not on a night when it was a good twenty degrees below Fahrenheit; they had to keep warm too. I eased my way up the trail to where the ditches were steepest and switched my truck off so that I could listen. I could hear their vehicle still running, I could even hear them talking although there was no way I could make out what they were saying. You know that "curiosity killed the cat" thing? Well that applied to me that night; I had to have a look. I walked down the trail a couple of truck lengths when, oh crap, here they were driving towards me ,head lights on. I turned at once and ran madly back to my vehicle. When they appeared around the large clump of scrub just ahead, I would put my lights on. That way, they would be caught between the ditches, their only escape route being to back up in one heck of a hurry, unlikely given the conditions.

On they came, lights on, apparently not a care in the world. I switched my lights on. It was really neat, their faces registered major surprise. Although the adrenalin was pumping, it was time to be cool. Hello, what was this on the truck door? Uh huh, the logo of the provincial power company...... now that would make my job a lot easier. It gave me what is called "leverage", although I was not sure the driver was fully aware of that yet. There appeared to be three of them in the truck as far as I could make out, evidently fully prepared to brazen it out judging by their attitude.

"Hi fellahs," I greeted them affably. "How are you doin'?"

"Great," responded the driver. "It's okay, we have a tag."

"Uh huh, I'm sure you do," I said. "Do you mind showing it to me?" That was when one of the passengers chimed in.

"I shot and tagged the moose this afternoon, officer, but it was too stinkin' big to get into my buddy's vehicle. So we decided to come back with his truck, and that's why we are here," he finished lamely.

"Let's take a look then," I said. We all climbed into the back of the truck to view the tag that had suddenly appeared quite by magic since I had last seen the animal. Better still, the tag number actually matched the fellow's licence. So far, so good for them, but the events of the afternoon suggested that some lying was going on. The question was, who was doing the lying? I decided to take the driver to one side; since he was the one who had the most to lose, he might be the one who would grasp the reality of their rather tenuous situation.

"By the way, you should know that most companies do not allow their vehicles to be used for hunting purposes. They get a bit peeved when their trucks get impounded because of the extra-curricular activities of their employees." To his credit, the man was not long at seeing the light. "You see, I happen to know that this moose was not tagged this afternoon." I pulled out my notebook with perhaps a little more drama than was necessary. "Aha! It says here that I came upon a dead moose at two o'clock this afternoon. No tag, no nothing. So I slit the ears and carved my initials in the roof of its mouth. Let's take a look, just so that you know what evidence I shall be presenting in court."

We climbed back into the truck and took a look at the ears and the inside of the mouth. Wouldn't you know it, this act prompted a whole new round of storytelling.

"Actually, it's like this, officer, and I am not lying. I was doing my rounds for the power company this afternoon when I saw the moose. It was a damn fine one as you can see, so I shot it. But I had already shot a moose using up my own licence and tag . That's when I decided to get my buddy to come out with me and tag it for himself. He had a licence and tag that he had not used yet. By the way," he signaled the other two over, "this is Zeke and this is his sidekick, Clem."

"Pleased to meet you." I was careful not to sound too smug. But my strategy was obvious. Since Zeke had not heard what the driver had said, a short interview with him would doubtless prove interesting. Moreover, Zeke seemed a little tense and was acting suspicious. Still, he was the guy with the licence and the tag after all. Maybe it was just that he was horribly unaware of what had passed between me and the driver. He handed his licence over when I asked.

"Okay," I said. "By the way, can I see your driver's licence?" Well, that caused the tension to rise a notch or two, let me tell you. He handed over his licence.

"What's this?" This is not the same name that is on the licence for the moose. How can this be?" I got one of those looks, one of those "who's this blankety blank in uniform" looks, in reply.

"Well, to tell you the truth, the moose licence belongs to another friend. He couldn't come with us because he is baby-sitting for his wife who has gone out for the evening."

I don't need to tell you that this was turning out to be a true ticket bonanza. I allowed then that the moose was now under seizure since it was not tagged immediately, and a licence shown was not being carried by the person named thereon. Eventually, realizing the gravity of their situation, the men reluctantly helped me transfer the moose from their

16

truck to mine, quite a job since it had not yet been gutted so it had to weigh around six hundred pounds. One has to be careful in this kind of situation. As people start to mull over what has happened, some people's quiet demeanor can change dramatically and they become tempted to do something at your expense, no matter how much they might regret it later. Certainly the fellow with the baby-sitting buddy was very agitated making me very wary of getting too close to him. Hunters have easy access to weapons, not just rifles but knives and so on.

Then came the fun part. Who should get what ticket? There was "hunting without a licence", "carrying the licence of another", illegal possession of wildlife, "allowing another to use ones licence". This last player I still had to find but I had his name and address. It is easy for a Fish and Wildlife Officer to go easy on poachers in these circumstances, but if you do not prosecute the consequences of illegal activity, there would be nothing but a free-for-all out there in the bush. So it was tickets all round; they were all charged and skulked away from the scene sadder but wiser men. I left as pleased as punch, albeit with a pile of paperwork as long as my arm.

Ah, but the story is not yet over! Oh no!

There were the court appearances that went along with the tickets. I've heard it suggested many times that somehow, if a well-turned out lady is recruited to plead your case, you might get your fine reduced. I would not have brought this up had I not been witness to the court appearances of the poachers.

Some months after the incident, we found ourselves stuck in the interminable proceedings of court. The case was unfolding at the normal plodding pace and everybody was either trying to stay awake or thinking about lunch. One of the hunter's names was called. From the back of the court, we heard the click of high heels on the tile floor. Remember now, this is small town not just Alberta, but northern Alberta circa 1970. High heels were wedding dress, not court attire. All eyes turned languidly towards the source of this sound, then came alive in amazement. This was one fine-looking, well-contoured lady; she knew it, and she showed it. This was at the time when short skirts were all the rage; she must have attended the sale boasting the world's shortest. Indeed, there were many in the audience who were praying she would drop something. Her measured progress toward the front of the courtroom was the most closely monitored activity of the day, not a heel click was missed. She stopped theatrically, making very sure everybody could see she was tucked in and hung out in all the right places. It was so quiet, you could have heard a fly fart. Peering over the top of his glasses, even the judge was mesmerized, his Adam's apple making a couple of unscheduled trips, perhaps to quell his heartbeat. He struggled visibly to regain his composure and asked, "are you the person whose name appears on the ticket?" There was a general snickering.......this was about as far from a man as you could ever get!

"Order! Order!" Control had to be reestablished, and quickly. The lady identified herself as the wife of the accused. She was asked if she understood the charge. Yes, it seemed that she did. She went on to plead guilty on behalf of her husband. The fine was levied. And yes, it was the lowest fine of all of the defendants, although not lower than the minimum required.

You be the judge!

4 ~ RECYCLED CRANBERRIES.

How do you get a bear out of a tree? Not a deep philosophical question, certainly not one to challenge a warden. In most cases, our objective as wardens is to keep animals alive in the first instance, and then move them to a new location where nuisance value ceases to be an issue. I recall one occasion where it could be said Fish and Wildlife and a couple of bears provided all the entertainment.

It all began when we received a call from a distressed farmer who had just shot a female bear. Apparently, the bear found its way into his yard and was heading for his pigpen with what the farmer decided were obvious intentions; bears of all sizes love pork. Out came the rifle, down went the bear. Initially, our caller had not realized the bear was a sow. He saw no cubs to suggest otherwise. Nevertheless, he was unhappy he had shot a female; farmers also tend to be in the business of saving life rather than taking it.

Not long after, he found his dog making one heck of a commotion in a grove of poplar trees near his house. That was when he saw the two cubs. It was early fall so the cubs would have been somewhere around the 20 to 30 pounds in weight. Naturally, the bears climbed up the nearest tree, the dog snapping vainly at their heels. The farmer, already disappointed with himself for destroying the mother, now faced a further dilemma; should he shoot the cubs and have done with it, or should he phone around and see if someone might be interested in catching them and maybe relocating them to a zoo? Fortunately for those two little critters, he chose the latter. This was the point when my partner and I arrived on the scene. Eternal optimists that we were, we brought along our bear trap to transport them out in the unlikely event we managed to catch them.

"Good to see you guys," the farmer greeted us on his porch. "They're over there in those trees."

Actually, they were both in the same tree, and as we arrived, they chose to scramble up even further. As for the tree, it was a large Trembling Aspen in the neighborhood of 40 to 50 feet tall. By now the bears had made their way beyond the halfway point. Well now, what should we do? Ah, thank God for the enthusiasm of youth, optimistic at best, reckless at worst. My partner on this day was one of those men who prides himself on being an athlete, but to me his skills were as yet untested. Certainly his volunteering to climb up the tree after the cubs was above and beyond the call of duty.......but what the hell, these young guys always have to try everything, don't they? Besides, the cubs were not big enough to hurt him too badly, unless he got overexcited and fell out of the tree.

"Go for it! I'll watch." This day, my heart counseled me to be the realist and keep my feet planted firmly on the ground.

Any of you who have climbed up anything in the wild know how tough it can be! This particular tree had not one single branch below the 20 foot mark. Sure, there were some bumps left by old branches, and there was also a bit of fungus, but there was nothing any normal person could get a grip on. What to do with the bears themselves would be a problem worthy of consideration only after my partner had fully demonstrated his climbing powers. I have to confess here I did not think that he would get anywhere near them.

For something to do while Spider-Man was doing his thing up the tree, I developed my game plan on the ground. Sending the cubs down to me airmail from 20 feet seemed the most practical of all the alternatives. At the 20 foot mark, there was a crotch in the trunk, itself four to five feet around. Here the main trunk split into two matched sub-trunks if you like, each reaching its way up into the blue sky in competition for light. Both bears had chosen the right fork. Much to my amazement, my partner was turning out to be a far better athlete than I thought he was. But as soon as he had made it above the fork, those wily bears simply took themselves up another ten feet, the topmost one now baulking about going any higher. This enabled our hero to grab on to the hind leg of the lower one. Holy smoke, he had done it! And he held on! The good news was he had some strong branches both to hold and to stand on, and his balance was solid.

By this time, the bears were squawking and squealing and putting up a real ruckus. This hulk in their tree was a real threat, and every other time they had chosen to make this unholy racket, mother had come bounding her way to their rescue. Sorry kids, not this time! As my partner maneuvered his hand to get an even better grip, the squawking became hysterical. The cub then turned to bite whatever it was that had a hold of it. As its head came down, my partner's hand relinquished its grip allowing his other hand to shoot out and grab it by the scruff of the neck. Now that was really impressive, although his expressive language seemed to indicate that he had not been quite quick enough. For his pains, he got himself peed on, his upper body liberally sprayed with a shower of bright yellow, but he held on! And that was when I knew we were the entertainment: a tremendous wave of laughter swept over us. I turned to find that the farmer had very kindly invited over all of his neighbors to watch the shenanigans. Being occupied in clearing a landing site for the airmail aspect of our enterprise, no pointed sticks nor jagged rocks that might damage our fragile packages, I had not noticed the gradual accumulation of spectators. Still, for my part I was comfortable with the idea that a 20 pound package "posted" from a height of twenty feet, would not be in harm's way. By the time my partner and the cub had climbed down to the crotch of the tree, the drop zone was ready.

Finally, the package was on its way! If you have ever seen a flying squirrel, the bear resembled a giant one. He was spread out and lined up for the center of the drop zone, landing gear down but not locked. He landed with something of a "whoosh" as some of his wind was knocked out of him. I had dealt with these little guys before and knew they could give you a nasty bite if you were not careful. I pounced on him before he could recover and run. Instinctively he turned to bite my hand but I had him just behind the ears with my one hand and by the small of his back with the other. And so the small package proceeded on its way to the trap by runner. When I got back to the landing zone, my partner had regained his breath and composure and was en route up the tree for number two, now cheered on by the ever-increasing audience. That the spectators were right into it was evidenced by the ebb and flow of their reactions, the "oohing" and the "ahing" at the flight of the first cub, the wild cheering when the little fellow peed on his pursuer, the tense silence as my partner elected to climb the tree. On the other hand, it was clear I was no hero; I got absolutely no reaction for my super-athletic pounce, not even a honorable mention.

Back up the tree, great progress was made in going after number two. Having seen what happened to his twin brother, he appeared to be decidedly unimpressed. He climbed further up, gamely pursued by a partially winded game warden. Finally, I was prompted to yell at him that the branches he was using were getting a little too thin to be safe. I was dutifully ignored. He tried a grab, missed, prompting the cub to seek even greater altitude. Now I was really concerned about him falling, but he soldiered on. Another mighty lunge.......got him! The way those branches were swaying, I was certain that I would be receiving both of them by airmail. Now what the hell was that on his head? My mind struggled to make sense of this new development causing so much amusement among the crowd of onlookers. Cranberries! The bear had just crapped a huge load of half-digested cranberries over his pursuer! Down the extended arm they flowed, on into his hair, his face, seeking out every nook and cranny that they might seep into. Some even splashed to the ground where they were artfully dodged by me, the silent partner.

Credit had to be given where credit was due; our athlete kept a hold on that bear through it all, shaking his tousled head and spitting out used cranberries. The audience recognized his tenacity and cheered accordingly, so wildly, in fact that, I began to wonder to myself if there was some inner meaning. Were they cheering because the game warden did not lose his grip, or were they cheering because a game warden got crapped upon? Certainly, there had to be a component of the latter in their supposed adulation.

Time was taking its toll, our hero's strength was waning. He did his "flip-the-grip" change again and got down another five feet. Decision time; he could not come down any further without great risk both to himself and to the cub. That was it, down came the cub from about thirty feet. He and his little brother must have studied at the same flight school because their flight configuration was identical.

I made a small mistake on this one. He landed in the drop zone as intended and, like the other one, he had all the air knocked out of him. But since he had traveled further than his sibling, he landed somewhat harder. The result was that I misjudged his condition and failed to grip him as tightly and as close to the ears as I should have to avoid getting into trouble. Of course I was wearing a pair of leather mitts to protect myself from getting bitten. They were not enough. In a flash, he bit right through the thumb of one mitt. My reaction elicited a great show of applause from the audience. By now, I could have cared less about them, being as the bear would not let go and his teeth in my thumb hurt like hell, his version of getting even I suppose. Finally, I could stand it no longer. A quick punch to his stomach saw him release me long enough to let me get a better grip and hustle him off to the trap where his brother was making known his views about incarceration.

When I got back to the tree, my partner was lying flat on the ground, utterly exhausted. Yes, he did emit something of an odor; bear pee and recycled cranberries have a fragrance all of their own.

"Thank God, I don't have a good sense of smell," I said, dismissing the aroma with a chuckle. That comment came to haunt me a few minutes later after my colleague cleaned himself up as best he could before he climbed into the truck. The smell was indescribable, so bad in fact that we didn't just drive back to town, we flew back to town, windows down, my head outside of the cab gasping for clean air.

The two bears? Edmonton Zoo. As a rule, I tend not to like zoos but I hope it turned out better for them than putting them down.

5 ~ "NOW DON'T YOU WISH YOU HAD A HOOK ON YOUR LINE?"

When it comes to Fish and Wildlife , all the adventures start out fairly innocent. However, when you go looking for people doing things against the law, you can expect some confrontations. On one occasion, my partner and I were patrolling one of the outlet creeks from Winagami Lake. It was the season for spawning fish to be on the move, mainly Pike. This prompted a large shoulder-to-shoulder fishing experience of a kind seldom seen in northern Alberta during the seventies. On weekends, the participants were usually folks from outside the area. On weekdays, the local residents knew they could garner great success when there were no crowds. Our mandate called for numerous patrols as fishing limits were easily exceeded. The best way to monitor the activities of the fishermen was to patrol in unmarked vehicles and in plain clothes. My partner would position himself on one side of the creek and I on the other. We would then be able to get a good look around to see exactly who was doing the fishing and who was not. Then it came down to checking out those you saw casting out and reeling in a line, no matter what lure might be on the end.

It was time for our check. The procedure was first to try to imprint a mental image of the target angler's clothing in your mind and, whenever possible, to match that image to a face before making yourself known. Face recognition was always a problem because you tended to approach from behind, so clothing was the primary identifier. Once your presence and your objective was detected by the mass of anglers, fishing rods would mysteriously start changing hands. Parents would suddenly hand over their rods to their kids, wives would hand over theirs to their husbands, others would simply try to melt away in the bush. We never did catch all who were guilty, but we certainly ticketed enough to let them know that we had been there and we could show up at any time. Naturally, you would first check out your best guess as the person least likely to possess a licence; at the same time you would be monitoring constantly what the others were doing around you.

On this particular foray, I had targeted a big man who had been casting a large fishing spoon almost across the creek. I could tell he was the belligerent type just by the way he held himself.

"Good afternoon, sir," I said affably. "I am a Fish and Wildlife Officer and I would like to check your angling licence please." When he turned to face me, his scowl confirmed my first impression that he was something of a bully. My introduction had not stopped him from reeling in his line which suddenly burst from the water without any sign of a hook on the end.

"I don't have to show you any damn licence," he growled. "There is no hook on my line, see."

"Well, isn't that something?" I said. "But unfortunately for you, my partner and I have been observing all of the fishing going on for quite some time and we have seen you cast a number of times. And every single time, your line had a hook of some sort on the end."

He ignored this and returned to our initial exchange. "How in hell can I be fishing if I have no hook. You tell me that! And by the way, if it makes you any happier, no, I do not have a licence."

"Tell you what," I grinned. "If you feel that having no hook on your line after you have cast it means that you were not fishing, well that's fine and dandy. You can just go ahead and tell the judge why you think that is not fishing." With him mumbling and grumbling about "damn fish fuzz types who think they know everything," I wrote out a ticket and set the date for his court appearance. His rod and the line with no hook were seized as evidence.

Finally, the day of the court appearance arrived and the still surly fisherman was called upon to explain himself. I gave an overview of the circumstances for the Crown.

"Sir, how do you plead to the charge before this court?" the judge asked the accused.

He responded with exactly the same reaction as you have just read, and with the same sour attitude too. The judge looked over at me and then over the rest of the courtroom. Then he looked down at his written brief as if composing himself. When he looked back over at the accused, he tipped his head so that he was looking over his glasses rather than through them, and with a glimmer of a smile, he announced his decision.

"Sir, that will be a fine of one hundred dollars. Now don't you wish you had a hook on your line?"

No response, just the usual scowl from the fisherman. The titters emanating from the audience indicated the judge's humor was not lost, even though he quickly stepped in to reestablish order with a judicious glare. That judge was on the ball!

6 ~ SPEED LIMIT PLUS

Before I tell you more, I should start out by saying it never pays to admit what speed you were driving, even to yourself. To avoid outright lying, simply state the posted speed limit and then, and only if you have to, add how much faster you might have been going. Basically, what I am saying is although I do not find the subject of vehicle maintenance particularly thrilling, it does have its moments, especially in the context of the speed you like to travel. These moments take on an added significance when you drive most of your miles on gravel roads, or worse, for twelve months in the year. Moreover, everywhere you are required to be is at least one if not four hours away, and naturally it was intended you be there yesterday. A 1960 half ton short box , six cylinder, two wheel drive Chev never quite cut it. Add an extended deck into the truck box to accommodate a double track snowmobile, and you are about maxed out before you start. Throw in a couple of trips to the border of the N.W.T., others to Peace River, Rainbow Lake, Garden River, La Crete, and Fort Vermilion, all at the posted limit plus your admitted 20 m.p.h., and always on a potholed highway, and immediately you have the fundamentals of "maintenance stress".

So you have just returned from one of those 60 mile per hour plus 20 miles per hour trips from the back-of-beyond. You pull sedately up to your house and stop. Breathing a sigh of relief that you made it home in one piece, you reach into the truck to grab your thermos. It's at that precise moment the front fender chooses to collapse down- on to the front wheel. Further inspection reveals a broken tie-rod end. "Uh-huh," you think. The part designed to assure that your vehicle travels in the direction that you intend is resting uselessly but comfortably on the ground. This fact indicates to you that, as of this very instant, you have no steering, something that you are reluctant to admit to yourself too quickly. It follows that it would be even more unwise to contemplate what could have happened at 60 plus 20, this in an era when people did not wear seat belts. When this happened to me, all I could do was to head into the house and marvel at how I had cheated certain disaster.

Tires were always a huge problem, particularly in the early days when steel-belted tires were never heard of. The fleet of graders maintaining Alberta's gravel highways always did what they could, but they too contributed to our misfortunes. They left behind what was commonly called "grader steel", slivers of steel one to four inches in length and semi-cylindrical in shape caused by the downward pressure of the blade on the road. These slivers were downright malicious. They would lie in wait on the gravel, ready to puncture any unsuspecting tire coming along. Innocuous in the hand, these little devils would work their way through any bias ply tire and triumphantly through the tube leaving you with yet another flat, maybe even the third of that particular day.

On one memorable trip to Rainbow Lake, there must have been squads of these slivers ready for some sort of action at various strategic spots along the way. My tires were assailed relentlessly. The boat trailer I was pulling boasted two tires flattened, and only one spare. I had no choice but to leave it behind. Two of my truck tires were ruined beyond repair, both spares having been called into service. And Murphy's Law dictated the local tire repairman cum salesman was off at some fishing derby far from town. How very appropriate! Oh well, there was only one thing for it, try for home.

Forty or so miles from home, there was a loud bang from the rear of the truck. I glanced into the rearview mirror. There, soaring blissfully away into the dusty air, was a gigantic chunk of black rubber. I decided that I'd better stop and take a look. That was about all I could do.   No spares left and a long way from home, this was great! About a quarter of the tread on the left hand rear tire had vanished. All the plies of the cord making up the inside of the tire were clearly visible.

"Well, well, it's a ten ply tire so maybe, just maybe I can make it home with the tread missing." I said it out loud, trying desperately to convince myself of the impossible. You must appreciate my sense of humor was not in great shape after having had to change three tires, and after I already left my boat and trailer behind.

I hopped back into the truck. I would give it a try; after all, I had always seen great chunks of rubber littering the gravel highways so maybe it was all par for the course. Only now I would get to experience what it was like to drive with one quarter of the tread missing from one tire. Boy, was it ever rough, a thump-thump-thump that jarred the whole truck without mercy. This was not too good. Maybe I'd better speed up a notch or two.

Forty m.p.h. Still major thumping.

Fifty m.p.h. Still thumping.

"Oh what the hell," I said. "There's still lots of ply where the rubber should be, I'll just give 'er."

At sixty plus ten, she smoothed out pretty well; but best of all, the tire lasted out the forty miles to the garage.

I learned very quickly it is an art as much as a science to get the most out of a tire hell bent and determined to deflate itself and your ego, when you are way out in the boonies. You acquire a new sensitivity to what your wheels might be telling you, you become resolved not to surrender outright to Mister Goodyear or Mister Firestone, and you develop a certain poise in carrying on business when you fully expect another tire to blow out on you at any second. On one occasion while traveling to Peace River, I just had to stop for a pee break at the railroad tracks just north of the Twin Lakes store. While I was out of the truck, I heard two distinct sounds. One of them I was expecting, the other I wasn't. The "wasn't" one was air whistling out of a tire at an incredible rate.

"Oh man, I've changed enough tires for now, I really don't want to do one more. Come on, come on, you've never had to pee this much before!"

Finally! A mighty leap back into the truck. First.....second.....third gear, motor screaming its way up the hills, pedal firmly to the metal, what else is new? Must be okay.....doesn't feel too flat.....service station pops into view. By jiminy, I'm actually going to make it!

By the time I stopped, the tire looked pretty well flat, but it was still hissing air. The repairman could not believe I had traveled that far, at least four miles, and still had some air left.

"What speed were you going?" he asked incredulously.

"Pretty quick," I replied. After all, what would he know about sixty plus twenty?

Coupled with the business of maintenance is the phenomenon of hazard. The roads we were called upon to travel were always hazardous in some way or another. We had the ever unpredictable weather, the idiosyncracies of the wildlife, the inhospitable terrain, and naturally the quirks of humanity. Add to the mix the foibles of every driver and you have the ingredients for plenty of entertainment, if not high drama.

It was in this context that I discovered tipping your truck over is not a good idea, not in any weather, but least of all when the thermometer is stuck right around freezing. There I was, bombing my way down a road surface that was nothing more than compacted snow, first cousin to ice you might say. Both of them are equally slippery, but it was not as if I was in any hurry or anything; I was actually driving along at a reasonable speed. That was when I found myself approaching as near a right angle corner as you are ever likely to come across on a secondary road. Then it began.........!

This was not good, not good at all, I was sliding sideways at speed. Okay, okay, I could correct for that problem. Uh huh! That had certainly helped, but now I was headed too far the other way. Whoa girl, whoa, hold your horses! Now I was heading backwards so there was nothing to do but to hold on and wait. The whole business felt as if I was locked in slow motion. The truck caught a ridge of ice at the edge of the road and started to tip. In a vain attempt to stop the inevitable, I leaned over the opposite way. Boy, that sure did a lot of good.......there I was on my roof in the ditch! At least I still seemed to have all the bits on my body I started out with.

I crawled out the window. I have to confess, one does not feel terribly dignified crawling out of an upside down vehicle. I surveyed the damage. It did not look that bad really, outside mirror wrecked, corner of the roof a little bent. But I did need help if I was to get her back on her wheels, and help was not immediately forthcoming. Ah, finally I was able to hitch a ride the ten miles into Fort Vermilion. When we arrived back at the accident site with the tow truck, we found ourselves facing the front of my upside down truck. . The sun was streaming in through the back window, bathing the cab in a mysterious amber glow. What the heck was that all about? It turned out that the fluid had seeped out of the transmission, liberally coating the inside of the windshield, the dashboard, parts of the seat, and wherever else it could register its gooey presence. Apparently transmissions are not built for upside down work. Nobody ever tells you such things, you always have to find them out for yourself.

Once back on its wheels, the truck ran fine. Being maintenance-conscious, I filled the transmission with new fluid before starting out. But I had to put on my rain suit to keep all the sticky fluid in the cab off my clothes. The moral here is you should never clean out your truck too diligently, you may not have your rain gear when you need it, notably in winter.

When you work for a government agency, maintenance is always a function of dollars. That function can get somewhat out of control if you find yourself under-equipped for the kinds of task you are expected to do. The story that follows is less about maintenance and more about persuading the powers that be you need to be equipped for your reality not theirs! Nonetheless, if you don't have the most appropriate mode of transport for the conditions you face, it gets stressful on the vehicle you have to get from A to B.

In the early 1960s, the town of High Level was very new and tended to be very muddy. Yes, that's right, muddy, the thick gooey kind that made you grow six inches if you walked more than ten feet in it. The streets were graveled, but the gravel disappeared as fast as it was put down, especially when there was rain. And it seemed that it always rained the most on Main Street, for it was always the worst. Sometimes you had to take the most circuitous of routes to get to where you were going simply because you could not even attempt Main Street. This was where my supervisor came into the picture. Fortuitous though it was, he showed up after four days of straight rain, that same supervisor who had been woefully deaf to my pleas for a 4X4, pleas that went conspicuously unheeded.

Upon his arrival, he had been able to make it to our residence with his station wagon, but that was about all it would be good for. After supper, he decided that he needed something downtown. It was not far to walk but it was muddy. My Fish and Wildlife truck was pressed into service. I was wise enough not to protest it was only a two wheel drive (I had a premonition my dreams were about to be answered).

Main Street was an unholy mess; in fact, I had never seen it worse. Naturally this forced us to drive around on those streets that were passable and that connected back to Main Street, a delightful exercise allowing me to point out to him I was the only one in town who did not have a 4X4. Finally, we decided if we really wanted to get to the stores on Main Street, we would have to chance it. With a 4X4, there was a good possibility that we could have made it the full length of main street; with a two wheel drive, not a hope in hell. Of course I knew that at the time- he did not! We started tentatively down the street, with me emphasizing to him that although it was not always like this, it was still fairly common.

"You've got to be kidding me!" he muttered, hanging on to the arm rest and wishing he had not forgotten his toothpaste.

This was the signal for the truck to high-center itself as if deliberately, both back wheels spinning uselessly in the air, the underside of the truck stuck doggedly on a hump of mud in the middle of the road. I did what anybody would do, I tried the forward-reverse thing, knowing full well that this was all for show. There we were, stalwart representatives of the Fish and Wildlife Division, high-centered in the middle of Main Street High Level for all to see.

Fate was even more unkind! One after another, three 4X4s went slithering by at various angles depending on the consistency of the mud and the competence of the driver. As if there to plead my case, every one of them had some caustic comment about how cheap Fish and Wildlife was that they could not afford a 4X4, and one of them gave us an additional gesture that supposedly reflected on our poor judgment.

"You had this planned, didn't you?" challenged the supervisor.

"Not true but most fortunate all the same," I said with a smile, making sure the point was well taken. Then came the coup de grace. "I'll have to go find us a Cat because even a 4X4 won't be able to pull us out of this one," I could not help but grin.

He made as if to step out and take a look for himself but had to draw back immediately when he realized that he was still wearing his spit-polished shoes. Not one to lose any opportunity, I began at once to bargain a pair of my rubber boots for a 4X4. This led to a series of earnest comments about budgets, demonstrated need, fiscal responsibility and so on. Finally I relented, giving him the boots so that we could set off together to find a Cat. Thankfully, the roads being what they were, there were lots around.

On the way back, the gruff-spoken Cat operator found a moment to ask why I had been dumb enough to go down Main Street when I knew I would get stuck. I framed the word "boss" with my lips without making a sound. At first he looked puzzled then grinned widely, eyeing my supervisor with a level of disdain. It was an effective message.

When we got back to the truck, I scrambled down in the mud, still taking as much profit as I could from our unfortunate predicament. I hooked up the cable, stuck became unstuck, and we were back on high ground once more. The Cat operator left shaking his head, knowing that his gestures were aiding and abetting my cause. We got what we needed from the store and made our slippery way home.

I guess I had "demonstrated need". A big, shiny, new Dodge 4X4 Dodge Power Wagon showed up some time later without anything further being said.

7 ~ LIQUID STORAGE

It was sometime in the Sixties, winter was in the air, had been since October. Minus 20 Fahrenheit had happened enough times to freeze the ground solid enough to allow the commencement of winter road construction and partial completion of traditional ice bridges at Tompkins Landing and Fort Vermilion, both on the Peace River. It has to be emphasized that frozen terra firma and water are both vital elements of the economy to the whole area; without the freezing temperatures, the expected volume of logs and grains could never be hauled by truck across the two ice bridges before the spring thaw. This story was related to me by a good friend and as you shall see, it would have been a shame not to share it with you.

A word about ice bridges. They are constructed by repeatedly flooding a predetermined section of naturally frozen river ice until it becomes thick enough to carry any weight that you desire to move over it. This means that the thickness of the ice could vary from one foot to four feet or more. It also meant the completion of the Fort Vermilion ice bridge in particular was cause for great celebration by some local residents because they had been without a legal liquor outlet from the start of freeze-up when the ferry was pulled up on shore after its last run that year. The sheer desperation to acquire some kind of alcoholic beverage was just too much to endure for some poor souls who managed to convince themselves the bridge construction was complete when this was sadly not the case! On one notable occasion, a half-ton truck carrying pumps on to the river ice to flood the growing ice bridge to its intended thickness was spotted crossing the river. Did this prompt some of the more desperate to jump to conclusions? You be the judge. What follows is a story about how not to mix alcohol and ice.

As they always did when they had finished flooding for the day, the work crew erected wooden barricades across the bridge entrance to warn travelers the ice was not yet safe and the bridge should not be used. But during the day, somebody had seen the truck crossing with their own eyes! As a result, that night, even though there was a blinding snowstorm, neither snow nor wind nor barricade could stop a man on a mission. He moved the barricades to one side, took his truck down the riverbank, following the now almost obliterated tracks left by the bridge builders. He had to squint to see the tracks going out on to the river ice but he knew that he would have to follow them precisely if he was to make it. Basically, all he could see was billowing snow and the slushy ridged sides of the crew's tire tracks in the not quite frozen water and snow left on the surface by the construction process. Traveling agonizingly slowly so as not to lose the trail fast disappearing before him, he tried not to be hypnotized by the blowing snow; nor did he dare try searching out the opposite bank. Fate was not with him this day; he lost concentration for a couple of seconds and the track he had been following so earnestly had vanished. He had strayed from it by mere inches but it was enough, his truck refused to move any further, forwards or backwards. No matter how hard he tried, all that he managed to do was to spin his wheels. His first reaction was the most logical. "This can't be happening!" he shouted out loud, as if shouting could change such an ugly reality.

Then he got out and looked at all four wheels, seeing nothing to possibly impede forward progress. Okay, maybe he was missing something, maybe it had to do with his driving. He got back in and tried easing his truck forward very slowly. Nothing. So he gunned the motor full bore, putting the window down as if his hearing the engine roaring would somehow will his truck forwards. All that happened was he could now hear his tires spinning uselessly on the ice. It is truly amazing how ones brain can suddenly marshal all the facts for review in this kind of predicament. Here he was, spinning his wheels on wet ice in the middle of a snowstorm on a half-built ice bridge with twenty feet of black water churning ominously only inches beneath his feet. Life on the edge does not get much better than that!

It was time to take another, closer look. Aha, so that was it! In the dim glow of his headlights reflecting off the snow, he could just make out what had happened. One of his front wheels had dropped neatly into one of the holes drilled by the bridge builders for their suction hose that drew water up to flood the bridge. Whether they were barely turning or spinning at maximum revs, the rear wheels could not propel the truck either forwards or backwards, not even an inch. All they achieved was the melting of the already thin ice beneath them.

"This is downright crazy!" muttered the exasperated driver. There was so little of the actual wheel in the hole, how could it not come out? If only, if only he had some sand..........

Okay, so it was decision time. The story goes that the driver was either too embarrassed or way too thirsty to make his humble way back to Fort Vermilion to get help. It had to be High Level or bust! Every step on the ice and snow grating like a rusty door hinge, he followed the nearly invisible tracks over to the other side of the river, headed up the bank to the nearest house and got himself a ride to High Level. By the time he had made it back with a tow truck, the snowstorm had passed on. Where they stopped at the top of the bank, he should have had a clear view of his stranded vehicle. Alas, instead of an image of his truck sitting abandoned on the ice bridge bathed in a soft moonlight glow, he saw a gaggle of people with flashlights and a host of vehicle headlights traversing the snow-covered river and the ice bridge.

Somehow our thirsty traveler had neglected to tell the tow truck driver he was stuck in the middle of the river on a partially constructed ice bridge clearly not yet open for travel. It took one glance for the driver to spot the barricades on his side of the river. Unfortunately, the details of the ensuing conversation are lost to history, probably just as well. What is known is the tow truck driver recognized a wild goose chase when he saw one and headed back to High Level.

Back to his own devices, our hapless victim trudged down the riverbank and out across the ice towards the jumble of lights. The air was clear and crisp, with the Northern Lights putting on a dazzling display in various shades of green. He was oblivious to it all. Where was his truck? That was all he wanted to know. Another curious onlooker joining the crowd milling around did not attract undue attention, so he was not immediately noticed, a good thing because it gave him time to size up the situation and listen in on the chatter to see if he could figure out what was going on. Everyone seemed to be peering into a vehicle-sized hole in the ice, precisely at the spot where he had left his truck he had to confess to himself. But what perturbed him was all the talk of a car, not a truck, going through the ice. Where had a car come from? Who would be fool enough to drive a car down here? He began staring into the criss-cross of lights and the moonlight, trying in vain to make out his truck. Maybe, surely, yes that had to be it! One of his neighbors must have come along and, seeing his predicament, had pulled his truck out and taken it home for him. One thing was for sure, it was nowhere to be seen!

It was at this moment his presence was noticed, so he took the opportunity to ask one of the bystanders what happened. Apparently the driver of the car had been following some old tire tracks on to the bridge and had managed to drive into a big hole at the edge of the ice bridge. This explanation left our victim wondering why there would be a hole in the ice when there had not been one just a couple of hours ago. It had not warmed up any, perhaps a meteorite could have...........that's when the mind-deadening thought came skulking through the crevices of his brain..........no, it could not possibly happen.............or could it? No, not a chance. Ignore that thought. Take refuge in denial.

This was the precise moment he overheard the driver of the car recounting how he had seen fresh tire tracks going down on to the bridge. Surmising the bridge was open, he had been inching along following the tracks when the hood of his car suddenly nosed downwards. In a flash he realized he and his car were destined to disappear into the river through an opening in an ice bridge designed to keep them out of that same river. Quick thinking prompted him to push his door open just enough for him to clamber out to safety on the ice before he turned to see his car silently and unceremoniously swallowed by the black churning water. As he surveyed the scene, he found it astounding he could have driven into such a large hole simply because the bridge builders would have automatically barricaded a hole of this size. He took a closer look at it and it came to him - there were no tire tracks leading away from the far side of the hole. Why was that?

It was time for our man to make his Herculean effort to stave off the moment of truth. He was singularly unsuccessful. The absence of his truck, the location of the hole, the lack of any tracks on the far side, all these facts conspired against him, laying siege to his mind. The more he thought about it, the more plausible it became. The ice on the edge of the bridge should have been as thick as it was where it had been flooded. However, where the truck had sat with its one wheel in the hose hole, all four wheels were exerting constant pressure simply by being there. Overall, the ice was not strong enough to sustain such continuous pressure, it succumbed to the swirling waters below, sacrificing the truck to the rivers inky blackness. The driver of the car happened along soon after. Innocently following the tracks, his vision reduced severely by the blowing snow, he failed to see the hole and in went his car, a second sacrifice to the mighty Peace.

It was the moment for victim number one to tell his story. The onlookers listened in awe of such an incident taking place; that a truck just sitting there could exert enough pressure to go through the ice and disappear into the murky depths of the river, then to be followed a while later by a car, was beyond comprehension. After all, this was a typically frigid night in northern Alberta where the ice of any river was supposed to be hard and unyielding!

Well, the rescue effort would verify the story. A thick pad of ice was built to support a gin pole truck to haul out the vehicles if they were still there. Divers were hired to slip through the hole in the ice and locate them. They would then attach winch cables so the vehicles could be winched up through the ice. Incredible though it may sound, both of them were hauled successfully up through the ice and out on to the ice pad. From here, they were loaded on to trucks and transported to a garage for "an assessment of the river's wrath". I never did hear if either of the vehicles ever operated again: I have my doubts, seeing as how this all happened at minus 30 to 40 degrees Fahrenheit!

8 ~ THE WEDDING

As a Fish and Wildlife officer, sometimes you were required to go above and beyond the call of duty. Sometimes that duty tended to stretch the notion of "public servant" somewhat. On occasion, you could be called upon to demonstrate talents you never really knew you had.

In this vein, most people would never connect game wardens and weddings, except perhaps where immediate family might be involved. A game warden sitting in a cramped office with his colleague on a Saturday afternoon catching up on mounds of paperwork would most likely have been thinking about what time he could abandon this sweat hole and go home. For most of this particular Saturday afternoon, my partner and I had been writing out the supporting documentation going along with the many tickets we had issued recently for angling offences. Saturday is also the day all the city folk choose to come out and go fishing. Usually they have been listening to the radio or the T.V. to catch up on the latest hot spots. Thank goodness , these people made it real easy, what with the need for their daily fix of information. When we sent in the report, we knew where the anglers would go because we were the ones who told them where the fishing was good, loyal and dedicated public servants that we were. It amounted to what the experts characterized as "a symbiotic relationship", one most anglers never appreciated.

Anyway, back to the office and the eternal follow-up paper trail to validate the tickets we had written. There was a sharp knock on the door.

"Get that Chuck, will you?" asked my partner. "Some idiot has forgotten it's Saturday. Either that, or he's a complete illiterate who can't read the sign that says we're closed. How the hell did he get into a locked building anyhow?"

I opened the door. Standing there was the local judge. This day, he looked positively streamlined for a judge; without his robes, he was dressed in a sports coat and tie.

"Ah, Mister Shipley," he said, coming straight to the point. "I need a best man for a wedding."

"A what?" I asked, dumbfounded.

"A best man. A best man for a wedding," he repeated as if it was the most normal thing in the world. "And they're waiting," he added, a note of impatience already creeping into his voice. Needless to say, everybody in the room was all ears for a further explanation, especially from a man not known for practical jokes let alone a wacky sense of humor. There was none.

I gave in to my curiosity. "I'll go," I said simply.

Immediately the judge turned on his heel. "Follow me," he barked, obviously very intent on getting what he was doing over with. He led the way down the corridor to his office and opened the door. He was right: they were all waiting. First, I recognized the judge's wife, evidently playing the role of maid of honor, witness, and whatever else was called for on this solemn occasion. She was standing next to a decidedly underdressed groom, a fellow certainly not attired for a formal wedding. Next to him stood an attractive young lady who must have swallowed a water melon seed that had germinated. I was not convinced a Fish and Wildlife uniform lent any more decorum to the ceremony, but mine was not to reason why. I stood where instructed.

The ceremony began, the judge taking himself seriously and droning on through his part. There were a few scattered "I dos" and then a ring appeared from somewhere and it was suddenly all over.

"Thank you, Mister Shipley," said the judge somberly. "We're much obliged."

"Yes, thank you," echoed the groom, now all eyes for his new bride.

"What, no cake?" I thought to myself. Did I not deserve something for looking so good in my uniform? I headed back to the office knowing that I would face a barrage of questions. Of course, I made the most of them with my wonderful powers of exaggeration, not that the story took long to tell, which meant we were very quickly back into that humdrum ticket thing.

Another knock on the door.

"Not again," grumbled somebody. "Tell 'em to come back on Monday."

What the hell was going on? Nobody ever bothered us on Saturdays. I sighed and opened the door. It was the judge. Without the slightest trace of a smile, he handed me twenty-five dollars in cash for the best man job. I could not stop myself wondering if his wife got paid as well.

"Mister Shipley, you're in luck," he intoned. "Unscheduled weddings are charged out at a higher fee than normal. Have a good day." He turned to emphasize the conversation was now over.

"Whatever will be next?" I thought.

9 ~ A NIGHT OUT OF HELL

I awoke with a start. What time is it? One thing for sure, it's still dark outside. Two o'clock in the morning. Nothing, just dead silence. But then I hear it . What the hell is it? What the hell is going on? Befuddled brain finally identifies a motor, and it's roaring. What's more, the roaring is just outside of my house. Who the hell would come round here at this ungodly hour in the morning and make a commotion like that? It's enough to wake the dead!

Out of bed I go and run over to the kitchen window. My God, it's a cop! What on earth does he want? Yes, the cops and I see each other lots, but never unannounced at 2 a.m.!

I open the door like a wide-eyed kid. In a kind of surrealist haze, I hear him say, "quick, grab your shotgun and pistol. A couple of our guys are in trouble."

I hurry back in and get dressed. It's fall so it's already starting to get pretty cool. Besides, since it might be a waiting game, I decide to dress warmly. All this commotion had woken up my wife . I tell her what I know and that I'll be back "sometime". With that, I grab my shotgun, the version with the short barrel, and I'm out the door in a flash. Guess where my pistol is? In a thousand pieces on my workbench being cleaned. So much for that! I jump into the police car ready for action.

This is neat, the adrenalin is really pumping. It seems that two of the officers answered a call to a domestic dispute. A firearm is involved. The lone male implicated is holding a 30-30 carbine rifle under his chin and threatening to shoot himself if anybody comes near him, or if anybody tries to leave. Luckily, his wife and kids managed to make it out; it was she who called the police. I have to point out here this was in the days before SWAT teams and rapid response provisions of any version except your own.

At any rate, I'm informed that all the detachments in the area have been notified, the nearest being at Fort Vermilion, one hour away. The second nearest is Manning, at least an hour and a half away, while the one at Peace River is almost out of the picture at a good two and a half hours away. This encourages me to tell myself the whole thing is going to be over before anybody of major importance shows up.

As we head for a trailer in the industrial area where the incident is currently taking place, I make it my business to get the full story. En route, we also decide a silent stealthy approach would work best. We will arrive on site remain inconspicuous, watching and waiting. The noise from the car's engine is deafening but I haven't got the heart to tell the driver he ought to change gears, not when he's as nervous as he is!

Three blocks away, we switch off the headlights as there's still plenty of light from the moon and street lights to drive and walk by. We park the car at the side of the road leading into the general area. In those days, trailers were aptly constructed for such situations because the walls were thin, all the better for hearing, and all the doors were on the same side, all the better for watching.

We get as near to the trailer as we dare, all the time maintaining good cover between it and ourselves. Finally, we stop to listen. There is the unmistakable sound of voices, one very loud, others softer and more soothing, but nothing is intelligible. We continue to wait and listen, which is about all we can do in the circumstances. Nothing changes despite the fact that the incident has gone on for over two hours. Eventually, we decide to position ourselves closer to the doors. We belly-crawl from where we are to a location under a truck nearer the trailer, taking cover behind its rear tandem axle. I take the left, my partner takes the right so if there are any gunshots, we should be able to reach our respective doors hopefully in time to do some good. I move further out to the left, finding yet another set of tandems to hide behind. I am truly thankful to have a truck to lie under with it's wheels for protection !

More watching, more waiting, more mumblings and murmurings from the trailer.

Oh no! Someone is coming down the road behind us. He's sure going slow. The last thing we need right now is for someone to spook the hostage-taker inside. Hold on a minute! Oh great, it's another cop in his private car. He spots me but keeps on driving, without doubt intending to hide his vehicle further down the road. Within minutes, he's back with a rifle. He crawls over to my position to get the scoop on what is happening. I tell him what I know and then he's off on his hands and knees over to the other cop, and together they set about devising a plan of action. He's been gone a good ten minutes and I'm beginning to get curious as to what kind of "plan" they could possibly come up with so nobody would get shot.

BANG!

In an instant, I'm up and running for the door. I see the two cops doing the same thing. Let me tell you, you cannot imagine what goes on in your head when you do something like this.

Am I going to make it to the door?

Who's shooting?

Will that be the only shot or will there be another?

More to the point, if the suspect sees me running to his door, will he shoot?

Maybe I'll get shot with a stray bullet!

You should have let somebody else go first.

What the hell am I doing here anyway?

I'd better darn well make it, I've got a wife and two kids to support.

Suddenly the door flies open. I skid to a halt pointing my shot gun at the opening door. Two uniformed policemen appear, pushing before them a handcuffed prisoner. Doesn't seem as if they have any extra holes in them, and there is no sign of blood, so where did the bullet go?

"Everyone is okay," the one cop announces blandly.

"Very fortunate," I think to myself. So who did the shooting and where did the bullet go?

The one policeman escorts the prisoner to their car and leaves. We join the other officer inside for a re-enactment. The two of them had responded to the domestic call as they would normally. They went in to talk to the husband. Even to this day, I'm not clear how the rifle showed up on the scene, and in the husband's hands. But I do know that the policemen finished up sitting on a chesterfield facing one very distraught husband sitting in a chair opposite. The problem was he was sitting there with a loaded 30-30 carbine rifle cradled between his knees. The ensuing threats to kill himself coupled with his total unwillingness to part with the rifle became the nub of the problem.

The unintelligible talking that we heard were the negotiations to have him put down the gun. While he was talking, the man would move the rifle with his one hand down from his chin to point directly at the officers, and then he would move it back under his chin. This was accompanied by threats to kill himself or one of the policemen. Soon, it became clear the negotiations were going nowhere and the overall tension was mounting. The trick was how to get the rifle away from him.

The continuous up-and-down motion was the key. If the rifle could somehow be knocked upwards and sideways without shooting the husband, or else downwards and sideways without shooting one of the policemen, the plan might just work. Taking into account the distance to the chair and how far the policemen had sunk into the worn-out chesterfield, any move was risky. But it became increasingly obvious there was less and less choice.

The constable began to work his way to the front of the chesterfield so his hipbones were supported on the sold front edge. He projected his weight forward, placing his feet back underneath him as far as the chesterfield would allow. When he realized he had done about all he could do, he sat very still and waited. The husband, as tense as he was, noticed nothing; he just kept on swinging his rifle up and down, constantly threatening everybody, including himself. Up to the chin, down to the police, up to chin, down to police, death threats to one and all.

Then down comes the rifle one last time. Up lunges the officer. Up goes the rifle, but not far enough. The officer grabs the barrel, forcing the weapon down at the man's side, the barrel pointing straight ahead. BANG, the rifle discharges, narrowly missing the other policeman fighting his way out of the chesterfield. The bullet travels through the chesterfield and out through the front of the trailer leaving a nasty hole in the siding. The first policeman wrests the rifle from the husband who is spun around and cuffed in one single movement. The door opens and he is pushed out. That's the very moment we appear.

Back to the station we go to rehash the morning's event one more time over a hot coffee. Then it's time to go home. That's when I discover that my poor dear wife has been worried beyond belief while I was gone. There is more than simple relief in her face when she sees me. It turns out she has been sitting by the window for the rest of the night without knowing a thing. In the rush, I had given no thought about how worried she might be. That's because I had always intended to come home. One such incident was enough though! It's much safer dealing with a discontented bear or an uncooperative cougar than with an unhappy specimen of humanity.

10 ~ NOT IMPRESSED

Lac La Nonne was a favorite hangout for anglers. The number of fish and the ease with which they could be caught demanded the close attention of the enforcement staff, otherwise there would be nothing left in the lake. Now it is never a very good idea to go out checking fishing licenses alone in a boat. Keeping two boats together, yours and the one you are checking is one thing. Keeping two boats together when you have less than cooperative anglers for whom you are required to write a ticket, is quite another; it tends to invite comedy or disaster, or both rolled into one.

On this occasion, the boss was sick so he got me to patrol the lake in his place. Trouble was, the officer with whom I was to work with was well-known to the anglers, and so was his laid-back reputation for leniency. He was one of those "I'll give you a break today" types that seemed to work under a totally different set of guidelines than we did. On this particular day, he operated the boat while I did the talking, asking for and checking out the angling licenses. All went well until we came upon a group of his acquaintances. Immediately they wanted to know what this young whippersnapper thought he was doing, asking to see their licenses and even having the nerve to write out tickets. They were informed by my now very red-faced and uncomfortable colleague that this was the way it was going to be from now on, and if they did not feel like cooperating, they could be arrested. That slowed them down some, but there was no doubt we left them feeling betrayed, and very angry. It just does not pay for any officer to get too chummy with the "clients" when it comes to enforcement.

The crowning glory of the whole episode was the thirty-something woman perched on the prow of her boat, skimpy top, skimpier shorts, fishing her heart out, almost literally at that! Obviously, she and her companions believed a major exhibition of her unmistakable attributes, above and below, would save the day. My guess was it had happened before, certainly if the attendant commentary was anything to go by. My partner's face got a whole lot redder as I proceeded to charge her. Interestingly enough, the most prominent of her features were hurriedly covered up the instant my ticket book appeared. At least this allowed for my partner's face to return to something of its original color. I was glad he and I were not called upon to work together again.

11. SOME NOSE

After every commercial fishing season, there is always a check carried out to see if any nets have been left out by accident and to ensure nobody has decided to continue the season on his own. This is imperative on a lake as small as Lac La Nonne. It so happened this particular year my dad was holidaying with us. I asked him to come along. Not deterred by the vindictive wind howling down the full length of the lake and directly into our faces, he jumped at the opportunity. A howling wind would not deter him, not my dad! There he stood unbowed, testing the wind like a beagle. Finally and with great authority, he pronounced there was a pile of rotting fish out there somewhere

We launched the boat. The old man was not to be dissuaded, he kept on insisting that he could smell decomposing fish. We set off up the lake, right into the teeth of the wind. Every once in a while, he would announce he had lost the smell but then he would gleefully pick it up again. As we worked our way up the lake, he kept proclaiming that the smell was getting stronger until suddenly he yelled "stop!"

"It's right here," he said proudly, "right here," as if emphasizing that he had done his part, the rest was up to me.

Sure enough, there it was! A net of at least a hundred yards in length and sagging with rotting fish, only the odd one showing a tail or a gill above water. Angry and sick at the sight of so much waste, we managed to roll up the net into a great big ball and sink it with a net anchor attached. Only then did I truly appreciate my dad's uncanny sense of smell. We had traveled a distance of eight and a half miles from launch to net. Some nose!

12. WHERE TO HIDE SUPPER

The phone rang.

Thanks to Mister Alexander Graham Bell, many desirable and infinitely less desirable activities have been triggered by that ringing. This particular call was from a farmer who I had known for quite some time. He was both angry and excited at the same time, which did not do much to help him get his story out. At least I was able to pick up the gist of what he had to say.

It seemed he had been out at the back of his house when a half ton truck had driven by, evidently heading down the "No Exit" road just east of his home. It was a truck he had seen many times before so the owner's name quickly sprang to mind. But what the hell was he doing down there at this time of day?

Oh, what the heck, this was one of those "live and let live" communities so he dismissed what he had seen and carried on with his task in the hope of completing it before sundown. He was pounding on a piece of metal when he was convinced he had heard a rifle shot. He stopped his pounding and listened for a full minute. Nothing. He switched on a yard light and continued to work. It probably was a shot, he thought, but the moose and deer season was open so shots going off were not uncommon. He finished up what he was doing and went into the house and off to bed. He was fast asleep when the sound of a vehicle and the glare of lights invaded his bedroom awaking him. The lights were vehicle headlights. He ran over to the window to see the truck he was sure was the one which caught his attention when it passed by just before dark. Since it was two o'clock in the morning, he decided against going out on what would probably turn out to be a wild goose chase, preferring instead to go back to bed, wondering nonetheless what the people in the truck could have been doing for so long out there.

Morning dawned on a very curious man waiting for enough light so he could check out the tracks past his house that would have been made the previous evening and during the night. Never had he been so frustrated waiting for sunup; like any farmer, he had the sense of being violated if people had been up to no good on his land.

Finally it came time to go. Proceeding slowly in the direction from which the half ton had come from at 2 a.m., he searched for tire tracks that might belong to it. Nothing, not until he got to the entrance of a newly broken field half a mile from his house. It was his field, yet there were tire marks in the dirt that did not match his. Now he was really curious. He followed the tracks along the edge of the field until they abruptly turned towards the center, paralleling the brush piles that ran the full length of the field. Continuing on, he discovered a spot where the truck had stopped. Looking down at the tracks, he could see a large area had been flattened in the freshly disked soil. Now what had done that, he wondered.

A closer examination of the ground revealed boot prints and what was surely blood-soaked soil with small bits of intestine, meat, and hair. His guess was a moose. Off to one side of the flattened area, it was clear that something fairly large had been dragged away. As he followed the indentations caused by the dragging, more pieces of meat, hair and intestine were evident. The drag marks disappeared into the nearest brush pile. It was quite clear that some of the brush had been removed and then put back; without a doubt, something had been hidden in there. The farmer reached up and pulled away the covering of brush to reveal various discarded parts of a moose, the hide, the intestines, the head.

"So after I found the moose parts," he said, "I thought that I'd better phone you. There's something about it that isn't right. I mean, somebody sure went to a lot of trouble to hide it all, didn't they?" But it was the additional statement that betrayed his true feelings. "O yes, I should tell you that nobody has my permission to hunt there, and that means nobody."

"Who was it? And who was driving?" I asked.

"You're asking me to stick my neck out now, way out. So when you come down, don't stop at my house. You know where the field is. I'm sticking my neck out here. The last thing I need is somebody hassling me for making a report. It was a half ton, same color as the guy has who lives four miles west of here. I think it was him driving too, but you didn't hear that from me, okay?"

"Okay. But you're talking about so-and-so, right?" I uttered the name, he agreed.

"Good. You'll see me go by in about an hour. And thanks."

As if I might need further encouragement, or perhaps clarification, he added, "you know he's working in town, down next to the bank, don't you?"

"You mean at his brother's place?" I asked.

"Yeah, that's right. I can never remember the name of their outfit." Maybe he was now just trying to distance himself from the idea that he was turning them in, from the idea that he was reporting an offence.

Every Fish and Wildlife officer has to be sensitive to any source of information; in this instance, it would be easy for me to disguise the fact my information had come from an informant. I would make out I had found the moose on my own initiative, that was if the information went anywhere! I jumped into my truck and set off. Everything turned out to be exactly as he had said. The parts proved to be from a cow moose; any edible meat had been removed. Somebody must have had a guilty conscience otherwise why would they have hidden the remains from the wolves, coyotes, and ravens? Why would they want to do such an elaborate job of concealment? For a visual record, I took a couple of photos, first of the drag marks disappearing into the brush pile, second what it looked like with the covering of brush removed, and several more of the boot tracks, the moose remains, and the tire tracks. A cursory look at both the head and the intestines did not reveal any sign of a bullet whatsoever. Maybe it was there somewhere but I thought I already had enough information without getting down and dirty. Then it was off to the suspect's residence.

His wife bluntly informed me her husband was at work in town. Okay, then it was off to his place of work. There I was told he had gone out and would not be back for about an hour. What should I do? Go back and talk to a hostile wife? Or should I wait out the hour for his return and stake out where he worked? I opted for the hour's wait, deciding to position myself down the street in another vehicle and maintaining a view of all the doors leading into the building. It was a long wait, much to my chagrin; one prefers to do these things without delay because one never knows who might be phoning whom. At least there were no cell phones!

Wouldn't you know it? When I finally went in and asked where the fellow might be, it turned out our man had already gone home while I was watching the building where he worked. So how the hell did he get back into the building first, before going home, all without my seeing him? The simple answer was that he did not; apparently he had phoned in to say that he was needed at home for an emergency and would return later. I shrugged it off and headed back to the man's house.

He was there, that was a relief! After a strenuous denial that he had been hunting moose, or that he had any moose on his place, I told him there had been a moose shot not far from his place. I went on to explain hunters had been seen burying the hide and the guts in a pile of brush. I silently thanked him for being smart enough not to ask how anyone could have seen what some hunters were doing in the dark. That's when I introduced the notion about a truck the same color as his, having been spotted in the area. Still no questions about the darkness nor about the poor light. Obviously he had decided to play dumb, working on the premise that anything that he said could be damaging in light of whatever information I possessed.

"May I take a look in your outbuildings?" I asked.

"Sure. Go ahead, be my guest." His voice was confident enough but his eyes were somewhat shifty.

First stop, a look inside a barn-type building. Nothing in there but a tractor with a number of bales stacked in its front-end loader. Next stop, two rows of wooden granaries not far from the barn, eight of them in two rows of four. Nothing in the first four, so over to the next row I went. The first two were clean. Hello, hello, why were there tractor wheel marks leading up to the next one? There was some thin plywood nailed over the doorway on the outside, this in marked contrast to the others which had all been boarded up from the inside indicating that they were probably full of grain. Off came the plywood to reveal six large congealed stains of some sort evenly spaced across the granary floor. The rafter above showed signs of chafing where rope had left the tell-tale message that something had recently been hung there. Well, wasn't this most interesting? Could these stains be congealed moose blood? Yet, there did not appear to be any moose hair, and that seemed strange considering there would always be some even if an animal had been skinned in the bush. Had somebody gone to the trouble of cleaning it up, somebody with a guilty conscience perhaps? I took out a sample jar and put some blood and hair samples in it, just in case there might be a question or two further down the road.

It might be a statement of the obvious but the next move was to follow the tractor tracks to see where they might lead. They led me on a circuitous tour around the muddy farmyard and its outbuildings, finally exiting into a stubble field through a gate at the far end of the yard. From here on, you could not miss them, they took me off in the direction of a very large haystack. My pace quickened with anticipation for I was convinced this was where I would find the moose. At the stack, the tracks mingled in with a myriad of other tracks that criss-crossed over them. Was this somebody's convoluted idea of confusing any would-be sleuth? Whatever the truth, I was left with only one option, to check over the stack.

Let me tell you, climbing a finished stack around fifteen feet high is intimidating for most farmers, let alone Fish and Wildlife Officers who prefer to keep their feet firmly on the ground. And because the stack was finished off so tightly, all neatly squared at both ends and the top, there were few handholds available, making all upward momentum very precarious. Fighting desperately for hand and toe holds, I was finally able to achieve eye-level with the top of the stack.

"What the hell, the damned thing looks just like it's supposed to," I fumed to myself. It was about a couple of hundred feet long and everything appeared to be uniform and tidy. I pulled myself up the rest of the way and found myself standing on the top and near one end. Well, since I was now up there, I decided that I might as well go for a walk to the end and take a closer look to see how well all the bales were fitting together. They were all fine and did not shift even slightly beneath my weight. I turned around and started out for the far end. Halfway mark, and still nothing. Hello, what was that? Near the end I was approaching, the bales did not seem to be stacked as precisely as everywhere else; four of them exhibited a distinct lean in towards the center of the stack. Was the fun about to begin?

With the removal of the first bale, my day was made! There, cached ingeniously inside the stack, was the hind leg of a moose. With the removal of another three bales, the rest of the animal appeared; so that was why there were eight bales in the tractor bucket! Suddenly my investigation was for real.

Did I say for real? Reality had suddenly turned pretty ugly with the realization I had to find some way to get myself off the stack without incurring severe bodily harm. I began with an attempt at climbing down as if I was on a ladder; that did not work very well at all so I decided to go express. I pushed off from the bales like a flying squirrel and landed on all fours on the ground. This would have been no place for "Candid Camera" or reality T.V. I straightened up brusquely, hoping that nobody had been witness to my more chimp-like qualities, and brushed off all the bits of hay on my clothing before heading over to the house. Now you and I both know my every movement had been under surveillance ever since I had been told it was okay to have a look around. Well face it, wouldn't you be watching someone who appeared to be hell bent on taking you to court?

At the farmyard, not a soul, so I made my way down to the house and rang the bell. No answer. What was going on, I wondered. I knew for sure that nobody had left via the yard. I tried again. After a frustrating delay, the door finally opened.

"Yeah. And what do you want now?" Like wifey didn't know!

"Is your husband around?" I asked. "I would like to talk to him." I countered her open hostility with a quiet courtesy, guaranteed to get types like this even more perplexed.

"Just you wait here," she barked. "I'll go take a look and see if I can find him." With that, she slammed the door in my face. If she continued on visually attacking me the way she had from the moment she had opened the door until she had gone on to slam it, I would soon take on the appearance of having been ravaged by the quills of an angry porcupine, if I allowed myself to be intimidated by her antics.

Eventually the door opened one more time. "So what do you want now?" the man asked, the wife shielded right behind him but echoing his words and keeping up her own visual barrage. I found my sense of humor beginning to fade with all this mumbo-jumbo. Still, I kept my cool.

"You know you said it was all right for me to take a look around? Well, that's what I did. And I know you have both been watching me since I left here. I also know you can see the top of the bale stack from here and you both know what is hidden in there. You saw me on the top of the stack, at least somebody here did because I saw the curtains move........."

"That was the cat," snarled the wife, launching yet another volley of visual quills.

"Okay," I said. "If that is how you want it to be, I'll go and get my ticket book and start writing. I'll start with illegal possession since you people own the place."

"You've gotta prove it first," shot back Mrs. Porcupine, still not entirely aware that they did not have a legal leg to stand on.

"Uh huh," I said. "There is a quartered moose hidden up in the bale stack. It was moved there from a granary, and very recently judging by the blood on the floor of one of your granaries. This constitutes a major effort to conceal evidence from the Crown. Anyway, enough of a speech from me. You both know how a court of law works I am sure. We tell the judge about our investigation and then you get to tell your side of the story. Once that's done, the judge delivers a verdict based on the thoroughness of the investigation and the behavior of all the people involved, and that means all of us," it was my turn to look very pointedly at the wife. "Now I am going to have to call for back-up to get the moose out of the stack, that is unless you care to help me with your front-end loader."

"No bloody way," hissed the wife. The husband on the other hand merely shrugged his shoulders, stepped outside and headed for the barn. I followed, not totally sure of his intentions at this point. There sat the tractor with around eight bales in the bucket. At least he had the good grace to look a little sheepish.

"Are these the bales that you took out of the stack to make room for the moose?" I asked, testing the waters.

"Yeah," he said. "I guess it's gonna be an expensive moose," he added in resignation.

"Yeah," I said, deciding against taking the conversation any further.

He pulled the tractor out of the barn and dumped the bales. I hopped on the back and took a ride on the drawbar over to my truck. As I followed him to the bale stack, I noticed the curtains in the house move again but could see nothing beyond that. "Must be that damn cat," I thought to myself. However, if it was the wife monitoring what was going on, she would surely be about ready for one final charge.

When I got up to the stack, the man was waiting with his tractor. I jumped into the bucket and hitched a ride to the top, a whole lot easier than climbing the stack one more time. Of course a couple of "what-ifs" crossed my mind too. What if his wife came out right now and ordered her man to dump me into the sewage lagoon? What if he was the quiet psycho type and decided to take offensive action of his own? I could see the headlines. "F & W Officer Found In Haystack". But no, none of this, he was a gentleman. I loaded a couple of moose quarters into the bucket and he obligingly drove over and deposited them into my truck. I accompanied the last two down in the bucket, ever hopeful that he would carry on being the perfect gentleman. Yet I still had some questions to ask, if only to set the record straight. Illegal possession of big game, in this instance moose meat is one thing, I still wanted to know how he had come by it. I wanted to confirm that this was the same moose that had been reported as poached initially.

"So, do you want to tell me how you ended up with this moose?" I asked him casually. "It would help your cause if you were to be cooperative and tell me the whole story." Maybe he heard the word "cooperative", maybe he realized that something in the way of compensation for the behavior of his spouse would be useful; at any rate, he told me the story just as you have read it. Yes, and this of course was the first year he had not bought a moose licence, a bit of an oversight for sure. And he had done it all by himself, the killing, the dressing and all of that. The human footprints at the site bore him out. The moose had been shot before dark. As with everyone else who gets caught, he wished profoundly he had not done it.

I wrote up a ticket for illegal possession. Considering the eventual cooperation of the accused, and considering that he had to go back and face that wife, I felt this was more than adequate. His subsequent appearance in court resulted in a substantial fine. Moose meat went to the needy. Another day in the life of a Fish and Wildlife Officer!

13 ~ KNOCKOUT

Part of the business of patrolling large lakes during the commercial fishing season was the gathering of statistics to assure the authorities the prescribed numbers of fish were being taken. This provided the perfect pretext for the local fisheries biologist to satisfy his craving for a bit of action, if not fresh air.

On one occasion, we found ourselves traveling on double track snowmobiles from fisherman to fisherman, the biologist checking on fish poundage, I measuring nets and verifying licenses. It was one of those glorious days that give meaning to the term "the great outdoors", a day when things were going along smoothly with everybody doing exactly what they were supposed to be doing. We should have known better!

We came up to the next fisherman. My biologist friend did his statistical thing and I set about checking and measuring. He finished before me, and not wanting to hurry things along too much, this being such a glorious day and all, he went back and sat on the snowmobile. Being the passenger, he was positioned at the back of a seat. Finishing up, I placed my ruler in my pocket, knelt on the snowmobile in front of him, one hand on the handlebars the other on the starter rope. Knowing well that this beast had an abundance of compression, I pulled the rope with all my strength.

Owwwww! What the hell had happened to my elbow? Damn that hurt! God, I must have pulled it right out of the socket! Howling like a banshee, I grabbed on to my elbow and turned around. There lay the biologist completely motionless, spread-eagled in the snow. What the hell did he think he was doing? Was this some new game he was playing. Then it dawned on me. The poor fellow was out cold. And that was why my elbow hurt so badly, I had hit him full force on the right side of the jaw. I climbed off the machine still nursing an acutely painful elbow and walked over to see how he was. At that moment, his eyes rolled and he propped himself up.

"What the hell was that?" he asked groggily. "What the hell hit me so hard? Did you see it?"

I said nothing, just sheepishly imitated pulling the starter cord and held up my elbow. As he reflected some more on what had just happened, he started to laugh. That was the moment he realized his jaw hurt. The fishermen nearby had no qualms, they were standing there guffawing loudly like there was no tomorrow. Okay, okay, so it was one up for them to see these men in uniform make fools of themselves.

Even though we continued on our patrol, by lunchtime the poor fellow's jaw was so swollen, he could barely eat. All

I could do was to mutter a rather lame "sorry" and to suggest he not sit so close in the future!

14 ~ THE SNOWMOBILE AND THE FLAMINGO.

It has to be admitted; it is a good thing some people have to be up to something that might be considered as mischief by others, or some of us would not have a job or a career as custodians of the law. Trapping out of season was not something out of the ordinary. But sometimes making your way to where the trapping was happening and then making it all the way back often was.

On one occasion, we were alerted to some unusual goings-on near Steen River, just south of the border between Alberta and the North West Territories. Apparently, a trapper had started off the season early and so it was decided that we honor him with a visit. Just before we set out, there had been a string of freezing nights; it was snowmobile weather without quite enough snow!

My partner for the day and I loaded our faithful double track onto the truck on a very crisp morning. Although there was no snow to speak of, the frozen ground and the ice would pose no challenge to our machine. The trip to the reported trail in the "north woods" from where the trapper had originally departed was totally uneventful. Moreover, there was no indication that anybody had been there lately. This was not a great surprise given people operating on the fringes of the law do not care to advertise their nefarious activities.

Our journey down the trail by truck did not last very long. A large beaver dam on the downstream side of the trail had effectively flooded it, the freezing temperatures had seemingly done the rest, seemingly! Yes, the beaver dam was frozen, but how much ice was there? Not much! Was it strong enough to hold two men on a double track snowmobile? Unlikely. Our search to find another way to avoid crossing the ice was blocked by open water and hummocks of muskeg. It was always at times like this that theory would come to mind. Would the ice be thicker further out? Probably not. When there is a freeze and no shore ice and no current ice thickness may be uniform. We had to try.

Now the "how-to" aspect had to be addressed. We would get back on our snowmobile and head far enough back down the trail to give us a running start. We would then turn around and "gun it" so that we would be at our top speed of twelve to fifteen m.p.h. by the time we hit the ice. Here, we would veer outwards to where the ice may be thicker away from the creek mouth and then veer back in to the other side. Great in theory!

Actually, we were doing okay until we got to "center ice". This is not to discount the myriad of cracks emanating outwards from beneath our machine. It was almost eerie. Towards the half-way mark, I felt the rear end bogging down as it cracked through the ice. Darn it, we would need every shred of speed to stay on top of the ice enough to maintain forward momentum. Somehow our trusty steed powered its way back up and kept on going. Down we went again. My strident instructions to my passenger to get off were studiously ignored. Yet, once again, our snowmobile clawed its way back on top and stayed there. We had made it! Uh huh, that was the good news. The bad news would now involve how we would make it back over to the truck once our business was done. That challenge would have to wait for the time being as we set off down the trail after our supposedly illegal trapper.

Traveling on a bare frozen trail by snowmobile is not recommended. There is not enough snow to lubricate anything, external drive, track, and so forth to allow for a smooth ride. It does not do much for the bones of the human body either. Ten or twelve miles down the trail, we finally came upon a plume of smoke ; somebody was camped just off the trail.

Aha, there he was, the man we were looking for! He was with his family and another fellow who turned out to be his friend. They had a cooking fire going and a tent set up, just as one would expect. We asked all the requisite questions about the trapping, and then about who was who and what was what. Our suspect was entirely legitimate; he had accompanied his friend, the legal owner of the trapping area, and was helping build a cabin. He was not there to trap, or so he said. Who knew what might go on after we had left? After this anti-climax, we were still faced with the challenge of making it back to our truck dry and in one piece.

It was some comfort to arrive back at the beaver dam with the truck in sight, only now there was still a hundred yards of badly cracked ice to cross. We did some reconnaissance; there was no alternative, we had to cross that ice. This time though, the problems pertaining to a partially submerged snowmobile in two or three feet of water were explicitly outlined to my passenger.

"When I give the word, you get off the machine right now. At once. Pronto. Got it? You must understand that if you don't, we will sink, and then who knows if we can rescue our machine."

He nodded his full comprehension. At least in the direction we were going, if the snowmobile sank, it would be facing the right way for us to haul it out with the truck. And we had plenty of cable. Not that this would be much consolation!

On we got, did the "get-up-to-speed" thing and hit the cracked ice. Almost immediately, the back end dropped ominously. The directive to my passenger to jump off was given both loudly and sternly. Nothing happened, no reaction whatsoever. The result was there was no pick up in speed and any forward progress was slowing down dramatically. I turned around. No wonder, he was still there, hanging on for dear life. A colorful list of "expletive deletives" that would have embarrassed even the most hardened porn star persuaded him it would be in his best interest to get off. I stole a backwards glance to see how he had ended up, squatting, sitting, or lying flat out in the water.

Oh , spare me! Not here! There he was, standing on one leg like an oversized flamingo. His one leg was up to the knee in water. His other foot was propped against his knee joint. I could not help it, I started to laugh. Bad idea! The whole machine started to submerge only thirty yards from the bank. I jumped off now and keeping the throttle wide open, I pushed and cajoled that darn machine all the way to dry land. With the snowmobile back on solid ground, I could afford another breathless look around. There he was, still motionless, still one leg held up awkwardly in the air. You know what? He looked as funny this time as he did the first time. I shut off the snowmobile. Silence, sudden and complete. That's when it came to my ears, a plaintive pleading from this poor soul who wanted me to come to his rescue. Somewhat uncharitably, I reminded him of our little talk only minutes before and then I went on to explain to him that our machine had never been designed as a "flipping boat," and he was damn lucky we did not have to pull it out of the water.

He responded with some colorful language of his own, sufficiently muted of course, seeing that I still held the upper hand. Finally, he put his upraised foot tentatively into the water as if he was checking out a swimming pool for water temperature. Most folks know that if you have just driven over ice and cracked it, and there are chunks of ice floating loose in the water, the water will be hellishly cold. This made it quite interesting, even entertaining to watch him wade through knee-deep iced water. Initially he was picking his way very precisely past the slabs of ice but then the cold began to get the better of him; that was when he turned into an icebreaker plowing his way clumsily to the shore.

We left the snowmobile where I had stopped it and walked the ten yards to the truck, both of us making squishing noises all the way. We both had a change of dry clothes that we set down on the tailgate. Humph, no towel! Oh well, half clean coveralls worked fine.

Now the front of my shins had started to feel a little strange as we were walking back to the truck, but I had paid no attention. As I removed my boots and pants, I could see what was wrong. My underwear was soaked in blood. To avoid this ever happening to you, my recommendation is you not run beside a snowmobile in water that has ice slabs one to two inches thick floating in it. Incidentally, the other person in the story was the same fellow who went to sleep on the trail while hunting bears. You will read about him shortly. In my view, this incident made us even.

15. WATCH OUT FOR THE RICOCHET

Thunder Lake, now there's a phenomenon. It boasts huge pike, evidently big enough to be shot with a rifle! Usually the pike congregated on the west side of the lake in flooded grassy areas ready to spawn. Ten pounds and up, these monsters were never interested in taking any kind of bait so the most popular way to catch and kill them was to shoot them with a .22 rifle. This method could be very successful provided that the water was not too deep, you kept your big flat feet out of harm's way, and there were no rocks just under the surface from which the bullets might ricochet.

Generally, the spawning area comprised one or two acres with grass and other vegetation that was semi submerged in water from one inch to two feet deep. Otherwise the overall lie of the land was fairly flat with almost no cover. As if that was not bad enough in itself, we were also completely visible from the road, nowhere to hide the vehicles, nowhere to conceal ourselves very effectively. The best and only realistic approach was to play any situation by ear. We would also patrol the area as often as possible using a variety of vehicles to allay anybody's suspicions that they were being watched.

On one particular day, our persistence finally paid off. Some distance from the spawning ground, we spotted a truck somebody had taken some pains to hide. Maybe this was to be our day! Driving past in our borrowed truck, we noticed two men where the fish usually liked to spawn, and both were toting a rifle. So we did not attract too much attention, we continued on for another half mile. We stopped, got out to put on our waders, then split up as we had planned in order to emerge on either side of the shooters.

My particular assignment was to slip across to the opposite side of the road from the poachers using whatever cover was available. Then I was to re-cross the road and get as close as possible to the fellow who was currently standing the furthest away. We were able to get into some thin willow cover some distance from the suspects and position ourselves so they could not possibly see us. This left one major problem. If any of their buddies were to come down the road, they would see us instantly and the whole gig would be over. We were in luck!

We had just given each other the thumbs-up when we heard the yelling. Damn, they were on to us! Not at all; the shooters were looking intently into the water and hollering with pure excitement. Prompted as if by telepathy, we both started to run. As we did so, we saw the rifles come up and we heard the shots. Within seconds, we were so close we could see the fish actually double up as the bullets struck home, and yet the poachers still had no idea we were there. Clearly, they were so focused on the fish each one of them had, they were not about to pay attention to anything else. Both were trying desperately to trap their quarry with their legs and feet to prevent them floating away. Both of them were actually reaching down to grab their respective fish, at the same time trying to keep their balance while holding their gun arms out to one side to keep their weapons dry. Not only did this render them completely unaware of us, it left them defenseless. As luck would have it, my partner and I arrived at our designated shooter at exactly the same moment. All we had to do was to grab the gun from each shooter's hand and step back.

We were met with such a barrage of foul language, none of it could ever be printed here. What we found incredible was neither one of them had the presence of mind to let go of their fish, ten to fifteen pounds apiece. Naturally we appreciated that, every bit of evidence made our job that much easier!

I took the guns and went off to fetch our truck. The two apprehended fishermen were escorted back to the road carrying the fish. The guns were seized, the fish were seized, tickets were written, the old familiar routine played itself out once more. When we thanked them most cordially for carrying the fish for us, we were met with another diatribe of unprintable language. I guess they never thought for one moment they might be doing their good deed for the day on behalf of two game wardens enforcing the law.

16 ~ ME A BAD INFLUENCE? NO!

For some, a job with Fish and Wildlife represents adventure and intrigue, the kind of job men dream about when they are boys. And so there are occasions when you can't shake them off, those men who want to experience a little of the call of the wild, they absolutely have to go on some sort of expedition with you. Much to the chagrin of their wives waiting behind at home!

Actually, it can be very helpful if you have an extra pair of hands along for the ride, especially when you are running a one-man district. Naturally, it does not do you any good to put such well-meaning people in harm's way, so you have to be judicious in choosing the sort of activities that you might get into.

One fine day saw three of us set out in the truck, boat in tow, for Fort Vermilion where we would launch into the mighty Peace. We intended to travel down to the Vermilion Chutes, 45 miles down the river in our trusty 14 foot runabout with a 35 h.p. outboard motor. This would be the first trip for one of my companions, the second for the other. We were loaded with plenty of gas and the staple of any such trip, fried chicken.

The first trip a pair of us had made was not eventful, at least not as far as the level of excitement was concerned. It must be said often the most enjoyment you derive on a routine trip that you have done any number of times comes from the company of a good friend. Today, my one friend was nothing short of ecstatic; this was his first ever river trip, and it was to be on the largest rivers in Alberta no less!

Just downstream from Fort Vermilion, the dirt bank to the north side is Vermilion in color, hence the name of the fort. There are numerous islands of various sizes covered with mature spruce in the centre, trembling aspen next, and then as you approach the high water mark, you encounter several species of willow. Cow moose appear in healthy numbers on these islands where they go to give birth to their calves. Evidently, they feel protected from the wolves and bears, and any other predators for that matter. I am not at all sure they are right as on a number of occasions I have seen both bear and wolves swimming between the islands and the shore. On this particular day, we saw moose and other tracks but unfortunately no live specimens of any kind.

Regardless how many times you travel the river, the waterfowl population is always unbelievable, out of this world. The best viewing spots lie between the islands and the shore, not in the main channel of the river. There is always an abundance of nesting sites and food for all.

Our trip to the Vermilion Chutes took in all the highlights, the native campsites, ancient trapper cabins, that sort of thing. One of the old cabins close to the "Chutes" had something new to me, a roof made from bark stripped off spruce trees four to six feet around. This practice is carried out in the spring when the sap is running and the tree is in growth mode, making the bark looser than usual. The bark is then laid out like rolled roofing from eave to eave right over the ridgepole as opposed to running it lengthwise the way it is normally done. There were four to five pieces with an appropriate overlap to prevent leakage. Inside, the place was very basic, a table, a bunk, and a small window facing out into the bush.

We continued on our way down to the Chutes. It so happens that if you are in a motor boat, or if the wind is blowing the wrong way, you cannot hear them so the first time you make the trip, having a map and tracking exactly where you are can be a very good idea. Unless of course, you want to try your own version of extreme sport! Depending on flood stages, the chutes may be characterized as fast rough water or a sudden drop of four to five feet. In bygone days, when there was considerable river traffic both ways from Peace River town and Fort Chipewyan, you might have seen the Hudson Bay boats, among others, lined up at the Chutes at high water.

We had tied our boat up at a landing just upstream of the Chutes and walked down to the low side of the chutes to have a look. On this occasion, the water was dropping a good four to five feet. Close by the shore, some of the bedrock was evident, slabs of a gray brown color with good-sized overhangs. We broke off pieces about the size of an outstretched hand for souvenirs. After looking around a bit further, we headed back to the boat for lunch. Placing our souvenirs on the dashboard, we set about eating our chicken with gusto.

Now is probably a good time to mention "the bug". Actually, I should say "bugs", and as plural as you could ever make it. Ah yes, that inscrutable, non-discriminatory, ever-present nemesis of man and beast, the lowly bug. This may be a bad comparison but they are like the "scarlet pimpernel" of French folklore; they seek you here, they seek you there, they seek you everywhere. Suffice to say, any and all types of bug native to northern Alberta await your arrival at every outdoor location with studied patience and pent-up tenacity of creatures with a voracious appetite to satisfy.

Needless to say, they did not disappoint us when we arrived at the Chutes. Mosquitoes, dragonflies, hornets, wasps, bees, these were hardly worth a mention in the total insect/bug picture. There were many that did not actually bite but still strove to exasperate! To add to our discomfort, the numbers this year were at an all-time high. The continuous noise was one thing. The other, and far worse, was trying to keep them off your food and out of your mouth. Unless you are comfortable with the unsolicited and instant colonization of your mouth by them, talking and eating with your mouth barely open is mandatory.

We were doing "all of the above", having had previous direct experience with the insect life and we had pretty good success. To our delight, a good stiff breeze came down the river, scattering all but the most tenacious back into the bush. A lull in the breeze allowed us a sight seldom witnessed. We were all looking over the bow of the boat, watching in fascination at the voracious dragonflies swooping and diving for all kinds of fare chancing their way. As we watched, and with the speed of a striking snake, a dragonfly caught a horse fly. Instantly there was a loud snap which we took to be the dragonfly breaking the horse fly completely in half. The best part of the incident was witnessing the dragonfly land on the prow of the boat to munch contentedly on its prey only three feet away.

During our shared lunch experience with the dragonfly, our souvenirs lying in the sun on the dashboard had themselves been busy. They had developed irregular dark brown blotches that were somewhat tacky and smelled like oil.......which is exactly what they were. Don't panic! This information was long ago recorded by both the petroleum industry and the government.

Following on from this, our return trip was very pleasant but quite uneventful. However, it seemed that I was construed as a bad influence nevertheless. The third member of our party, the one for whom the trip had been his first sortie ever on a river, was a close friend of my other companion. The latter had talked up this trip to such a degree that his pal simply had to experience it for himself. He had enjoyed himself so thoroughly that as soon as we landed, I was assailed by both of them cajoling, bribing, bargaining, whatever it took for me to invite them along on another trip. Being of gentle nature and reasonable disposition, I relented.

On the first trip, we had been able to make an early start and avoid mechanical problems. The second trip turned out to be a different affair altogether. This time, for whatever reason, we started out late. To make matters worse, the boat launch was covered with silt forcing us to cross the river on the ferry and launch our boat on the other side of the river. As if miffed by all this delay, the motor refused to start. More time was consumed while we installed new spark plugs, but eventually we found ourselves loaded and out on the river. Now we got into the spirit of things and stopped at all of our favorite spots from the previous trip; when you are having fun, the notion of time often becomes irrelevant. When we actually made it to the chutes, we tied up and did the "tourist thing", looked around, picked up some souvenirs and returned to the boat for supper. A hundred miles south of the NWT border, there was never any danger of running out of daylight in the last half of July so there was no urgency to anything we did.

Time to head home. Once again the motor was uncooperative, more trouble with plugs. Did this mean they were defective or were the oil and gas mixed up in the wrong ratio? Muttering an unflattering commentary, I replaced the plugs a second time and we took off. Additional requests to stop here and there on our way home were honored with no regard to time. By midnight, we still had some distance to go but nobody cared. Besides, anyone who has traveled on water when there is a clear sky and it is getting darker, or is dark already, knows that the darkness is never complete, not in this part of the world in July. The upshot of this is you can still see what is going on, not as plainly as in daylight, but you can still see. This was how we were operating that "night", hoping all the time that there were no submerged logs to end our journey prematurely. At last the launch site came into focus and we were on the road for home. Somewhere around one o'clock in the morning, we knew in a couple of hours or so we would be all back in the comfort of home.

Hello, hello! Why the heck were all the lights on in my house? One of the girls, perhaps my wife, must be sick. It did not take long to find out. As soon as I opened the door, I was regaled with the information that the distraught wife of my partner's friend had been phoning every half hour since before midnight, and here we were at 2:30 a.m.

"Her constant phoning woke the kids and kept me awake," my wife explained. "I finally had to tell her you guys were big boys now and that you could all look after yourselves." To reinforce her message, she had added the statement that she never ever knew what time I would be getting home, "so we'll all have to wait, won't we?" she had finished sweetly. Seemingly, the lady was not overly impressed.

Later, it turned out she had been phoning my partner's wife also, all of which left me with the clear impression that if we were to go on any further trips, the man's wife would have to have some direction, even counseling, as to how to conduct herself when her man was out with a game warden of such questionable reputation!

17 ~ I WAS WARNED ABOUT YOU

I have referred to Narrows Creek in other stories; it is west of the Narrows on Lesser Slave Lake and on the north side. A well-known haven to locals, it provided shelter from the sometimes vicious storms along a lakeshore offering little in the way of sanctuary. Depending on the level of the lake, there may be a sandbar across the mouth of the creek; hence it is always advisable to navigate over or around this obstruction with due care and attention. The navigable length of the creek itself is nigh upon half a mile, replete with sudden twists and tight turns, and that ubiquitous deadfall. Close to the creek's mouth, there is a campsite used by the commercial fishermen for both camping and the storage of equipment.

Whenever I had a change of officers on my staff, a day patrol along the north shore of Lesser Slave Lake was mandatory. Today was one of those days. We launched our sixteen foot runabout at Grouard at the west end of the lake, the idea being to give my new partner a blow by blow visual account of the north shore highlights from a Fish and Wildlife perspective. The Causeway at Grouard was our starting point. From there, we followed the single channel out to the main body of the lake, passing Shaw's Point with its multitude of summer cabins. Hugging the shore closely, we skirted Hilliard's Bay campground, with me offering a running commentary on where and when the commercial and sports fishermen could be found at different times of the year. I pointed out the small cut bank east of Hilliard's Bay, used as a landmark to locate a traditional hot spot for walleye. Beyond this, there was not much excitement until we came upon the small creek just west of Narrows Creek. Here there was a small house on the east side facing the lake. I recounted the story about the house and its occupant as it was told to me, a passing on of the local folklore if you like.

As I recall it, the house was tiny, about fifteen feet square inside. It certainly did not appear to be very old . When the waves came up, it was apparently close enough to the lake to get wet, as evidenced by the lake debris piled on the lake side. According to the story, an old commercial fisherman lived there alone. How long he had lived there nobody seemed to know, but the part that caught my attention was how he had died. It may have been during the commercial fishing season for that would have been the only reason a fisherman would have been out in his boat with nets. Again, nobody seemed to know. What was curious though was his friends found him out in his boat, dressed in his bathrobe and pajamas, his net half pulled, and as dead as a doornail. Somehow he had got himself caught up in that portion of the net still in the water and he had drowned. Since it would seem exceedingly odd for a commercial fisherman to go pulling his nets in night attire, the whole affair became shrouded in mystery, adding a touch of the inexplicable to the mythology of the local area. An investigation was launched but no further light was shed on the incident. Was it an unsolved murder, or something far less sinister? Even today, nobody seems to know, although there is plenty of conjecture!

My new partner was fascinated but duty called as we continued on. We were closing in on Narrows Creek, one of my favorite places at the time. No, the sandbar was not visible this day so we did not have to navigate around or over it with all the due care and attention that it normally called for, a pity because my companion needed to know how tricky it could be. The lake was high so we were able to idle our way into the mouth of the creek and land at the campsite where we tied up the boat. A quick look around indicated a recent campfire, some flattened grass where someone had pitched a tent, and a few empty fish boxes.

"How far can you take a boat up this creek?" asked my partner innocently. "It doesn't look very long, does it? It just seems to disappear into the bush up there."

"Yes, that's right. If you're lucky and there are no logs across it, you might make it half a mile. We'll take a look up there in a minute if you like," I added, my brain already scheming up a bit of entertainment for the day. While he was reveling in the novelty of his surroundings, I had a couple of minutes to secure our boat gas tanks and any other "loose cargo". To allay any suspicion I might be up to something nefarious, I suggested we first check the gas and then top up our tanks with the gas we had brought with us for the return trip; that way, there would not be any half tanks to secure. He was still pumped up with enthusiasm.

"Sure! Let's do it!" he said. "I would like to see where this creek actually goes."

"All set?" I asked jovially. He nodded. We eased our way into the centre of the creek and turned upstream.

"What's wrong with this thing?" he called out. "Why are you going so slow? I didn't think any equipment in High Prairie could go this slow!"

"Generally true, but sometimes there are submerged logs in here and I don't want to hit one and hole the boat." I laid it on thick and heavy so he got to thinking I was one of those senior citizen types, overly cautious and very protective of government property. At any rate, he seemed satisfied.

We ventured a bit further upstream at mid-idle until we came upon a cluster of trees that had fallen across the creek. There was no way we could slip underneath them nor around them, not that I had any great desire to try. Hell, it was tough enough to turn around right where we were because the creek was narrower than the boat was long. Fortunately, there was a low spot on the bank on the one side. We both moved to the stern of the boat and, pushing with the paddles, we nosed far enough into the low spot for the stern to be manhandled upstream. It was a simple move then to point the bow downstream. Since there was no current to speak of, I was able to hold the boat steady exactly where I wanted. We were now situated in the creek at a spot where it was ten to twelve feet wide, with banks of about two to three feet high covered in grass and trees some of which were reaching down into the water, the whole thing giving one the distinct impression of being hemmed in.

"You ready to head back out to the lake?" I asked innocently.

"Sure thing. I hope we can go back a little quicker than we came up though". I nodded.....

Little did he know how well I had set him up!

The creek had two switchbacks in quick succession, the same sort of twists and turns that one would encounter on any mountain road. In this case, we were required to start off straight, hang a sharp left only to then make an immediate tight turn to the right before a short final burst out to the lake, all within a distance of some two hundred yards. What I had planned for my partner could be best described as a nautical roller-coaster; the whole trip was to be undergone at near full speed, corners and all. But before I set off, I had to check first to see if any other boat had shown up while we were in the creek. Happily the entire creek could be viewed by positioning oneself on top of the front seat back.

"What the hell are you doing now?" my partner's voice betrayed a slight hint of anxiety.

"Who, me? Just having a look to see if anybody has arrived since we've been up here." Nothing, all was quiet.

I slid back down into my seat, braced my feet hard against the floorboards, and pushed my butt hard back into the seat; I knew what was coming, my passenger had no idea. There he was, so relaxed and contented, and so....... unaware!

"Are you ready?" That question was the only semblance of a warning he would ever get.

"Ready for what?" he asked gullibly.

In response, I gunned the motor, maximum throttle, seventy-five horses surging forward at full power. In two to three boat lengths, the boat was planning. We catapulted into the first turn, the boat keeled over so the water was lapping at the top of the gunwales threatening to swamp us. Of course at this speed, I had to start turning corners before I was into them or risk disaster. The effect of this is we appeared to be headed straight into the trees and grass dead ahead, especially on the first corner. There was no time to study my partner at length, just enough for me to catch a glimpse of white knuckled hands squeezing the life out of the heavily padded dashboard. One thing was for certain, he no longer looked relaxed nor contented. We flipped back to straight and level only to make a hard turn to the right, again stopping just short of submerging the gunwales.

Let me remind you this was all going on in a ten foot wide creek in a boat five feet wide and sixteen feet long. All he would have been able to see were three foot high banks coming at him and passing in a head on blur. If he had chosen to look across at me, he would have seen a madman at the wheel grinning insanely. He may have looked back, thinking his life was in order after the last turn, only to find himself careening into another one.

"The guy's mad, right out of it. So we make it around the second turn, who knows how, and here we are screaming across the mouth of a creek that he had warned me might contain submerged logs. And then he stops dead in the water and we settle instantly into a prolonged silence." The young fellow's story later was pretty animated, keeping his audience spellbound.

I just remember stopping, turning off the motor and asking, "Was that quick enough for you?" The publishers of this book would never allow his version of the English language in a family book such as this. That was when we decided to continue up to the Narrows for a look around.

Just to the west of the Narrows, on the north side, there were old rundown uninhabited cabins. The best part of them now was their setting, a light sandy-colored beach, 2 to 20 feet wide depending on the height of the lake, and somewhere near half a mile long. The southern exposure kept everything in bright warm sunlight during those long northern summer days. The view to the south was unobstructed for the nine miles across the lake to the dark blue hills of the horizon on the other side of Faust Bay. Judging by the amount of discarded fishing gear in the cabins and surrounding area, commercial fishermen had spent considerable time here. The cabins themselves still boasted some of the niceties of life but on the whole they were pretty austere; some shelves, a stove, the odd stray dish but very little else. For some, there was no glass left in the single window, others had a piece of plastic nailed across where the window should have been. Certainly, you could tell the people who had lived there had not had to carry everything on their backs; there were dozens and dozens of long-necked beer bottles. Since short stubby bottles were now in vogue, these others could be characterized as historical artifacts, part of a bygone era. The area was also a haven for avid blueberry pickers, which in turn would have warned you to keep a sharp lookout for the ever-present black bear.

"You ready for another river trip?" I asked.

"Don't think you'll ever do that to me again," was the immediate response. "Next time, I'll be ready for your antics. I was warned about you but at the time I just couldn't see it. You seemed so, so normal. Now I know better," he paused. "But you know what? It was neat. You must have practiced that a few times otherwise we'd still have been way up there in the bush. I don't see any river mouths around here, so what river are you talking about?"

"Just across the Narrows on the south shore, the Swan river comes in. It's a little tough to get into if the water is low but we can go and take a look if you like."

"Sure. Let's go. It doesn't look that far."

"It isn't. We just have to go a round a little point of land to the east of the Narrows on the south side to find the river mouth." I continued on with my orientation. "While we are crossing the Narrows, we are in the deepest part of the lake. It has been sounded to right around a hundred feet deep, very deep for this lake. During open water commercial fishing season, there are lots of nets set here and catches tend to be pretty good. Has to be that ever-present current between east and west moving so much food around that attracts the fish.

"That's pretty interesting," my companion responded. "So there have to be bigger anchors on the nets set here, right? Because of the stronger current I mean." It was refreshing to have such a receptive audience, though it forced me to think back a while.

"You know, we pulled a bunch of nets from here a few years ago and I don't remember if the net anchors were any bigger than normal."

We continued on across the Narrows at a southeast tack, finishing up on the south shore just east of the spot where the Swan River empties into the lake. As always, it was difficult trying to locate the right channel to take us from the lake into the river; after much searching, some running aground, and a bit of cussing, we eventually found our way. You guessed! We followed the river upstream through the marsh and willow flats at IDLE SPEED. It really would have been a long walk back to the truck from here. We got as far as the river's first direct connection with civilization where it came close to a north-south road. I pointed out the very small creek could be used as a launch location to the main river, preferably only if one had to.

"Don't launch from here," I emphasized, "unless you have some sort of emergency. There is no secure place for your truck and if it ever rains, look out! Even with four-wheel drive, you will have trouble getting out. Worse still, when it is storming on the lake, it is nearly impossible finding the mouth of the river at the delta if you have to come back this way. You saw how much trouble we had finding it on a good day like today."

"Makes sense to me. Which way are we going back? On this side, or back across the Narrows?"

"From the mouth of the river back across the Narrows is around twenty miles. If the water stays fairly calm, that'll be a little over an hour. The south shore route would be a lot further unless we go up the middle of the lake. But if a storm decides to blow in while we are en route, we would have to avoid it by following the north shore. To patrol the south shore properly will take a lot more time than we have today anyway, so let's go to the north shore." There was no argument.

Since we had entered the Swan River, the wind had come up causing minor waves that slowed us up a little. That was no problem, it was the ominous black cloud bank forming in the west that had me concerned.

"We may have a longer trip than I thought," I warned my partner. "Past experience tells me that there'll be some big waves before we get back to the truck, those kind of clouds are a dead give away."

"There's not much we can do about that, is there, other than keep going?" responded my companion. "That sure is an ugly cloud though." The next question betrayed a little apprehension on his part. "What size are the biggest waves you have seen out here? They must get pretty darn big if the lake is this deep."

"Well, again talking only from my own experience, there is often a good deal of imagination that goes into any discussion of wave height. My guess would be that the biggest wave might come in at six or seven feet. Some folks around here will tell you ten feet but I have never seen anything that big." As if to prove a point, both the wind and the height of the waves began to increase.

We stayed out from shore seventy-five to one hundred and fifty yards from depending on the aggressiveness of the waves and our quartering angle to them. I had long ago learned that quartering into the waves at an angle lessens their impact on a boat and its passengers and allows what I always hanker for, more speed. Our supposed hour-long trip back to Grouard was going to run to an hour and a half at best, two hours or more at worst.

The moment we rounded Shaw's Point, we were assailed by the full force of a storm we watched develop from almost nothing, a storm giving us a foretaste of its potential power as it buffeted us on our journey since crossing the Narrows. But now the wind from the west was unobstructed, blasting its way from west of Buffalo Bay, across the bay itself and the low land to the south, and down the channel connecting to Lesser Slave Lake. As if to add icing to the cake, there was now a driving rain making it more of a guess as to where Grouard and our truck might be.

For the next unobstructed mile, the waves gradually doubled in size, some smashing their way over the bow and the windshield, soaking everything in the boat. Not like the rain was not doing a good job of that already! Fortunately for us, the water here was not as deep as elsewhere on the lake so the waves tended to be smaller and choppier rather than the big rollers out on the main expanse of water. Nevertheless, they were still in the two to three foot range, enough to rattle our boat and our bones, and to pound our muscles into jelly. Through the nearly impenetrable screen of rain, wind, and wave, we finally spotted the channel mouth, just an anonymous hole among the cat tails, but oh so welcome.

No bad guys, a bit of fun, a little adventure, a touch of rough water, all pensionable service!

18 ~ CHASE THAT PLANE!

Throughout one winter, there were rumors about fishing limits not being respected at Beatty, Thurston, Bistcho and Esk Lakes. In the late sixties, accessing all these lakes situated in the north-west corner of Alberta with anything other than a ski-equipped aircraft indicated a long and arduous ride by snowmobile. In some winters, cleared seismic lines allowed truck access to some of the lakes, but never to all of the lakes simultaneously, and certainly not in this particular year. The complaints had become serious enough that I had taken my truck and snowmobile and attempted my own version of getting to the lakes. The only one I could reasonably get to was Bistcho, and of course there was nobody there by the time I made it to the north shore. This after driving down through Steen River,west to the Petiot River, unloading my snowmobile and following the river down to the lake. Clearly there was a great deal of fishing activity out from the mouth of the Petiot, between there and Caribou Island. There were fishing holes everywhere, but no sign of an angler anywhere.

Another week rolled by; more complaints. Finally I was able to convince my supervisor that a ski-equipped aircraft was required to take a comprehensive look at the problem. A flight with the local charter company was arranged for one·

Sunday morning. We boarded a Piper Cub with skis and departed from the airfield at High Level with a temperature at around 20 below Fahrenheit. On such trips, the vastness of the north never fails to impress; we flew for well over an hour over nothing but bush before Bistcho Lake finally came into view. From my co-pilot seat, the brilliant expanse of white, the snow on top of the ice, was simply blinding; we could barely make sense of what we were seeing. As we closed in on the lake, visibility gradually improved allowing us to home in on four short black lines near the narrows. This could mean only one thing, dog teams. As we got even closer, we could see clearly that the lines were on the move, dog teams heading east probably to a trap line. The trappers had undoubtedly stopped at the narrows to fish for the dogs.

We also noted that Bistcho was open at the usual location despite the continued minus 40 Fahrenheit weather gripping us nightly for over a month. The narrows between the east and west parts of the lake always seemed to stay open owing to a permanent current. This in turn thinned the ice surrounding the opening which allowed the local natives to set their nets through the ice without too much difficulty so they could catch enough fish to feed their dogs. Anglers did not usually frequent this part of the lake as it was not at all convenient for them.

Of course, I would have liked to chat with the trappers because they would have been the source of valuable and up-to-date information about what was happening in the area. Discretion prompted us to fly on; we really did not have the time and besides, we had no interest in scaring the dogs. I had been very tempted to land at the Narrows but when the pilot convinced me he could not get close enough to the net holes we had observed on our approach, I decided all I needed to see was if they had been recently used and we could do that from the air. He did a great job, tipping the wing on my side so that I got a clear view of the fresh drag marks from nets, even of the flecks of blood and scattered fish scales.

We regained cruising altitude and headed north-east towards Beatty, Thurston, and Esk Lake to complete our patrol. There was some stale sign of anglers having fished at Beatty Lake but not a soul to be seen. At the same time from our altitude, we could also see Thurston Lake, and what we saw immediately caught our attention. There was a huge dark shape out near the centre of the lake, a shape that eventually proved to be an aircraft. Okay, so we would hold our altitude and fly over, taking a good look at whatever activity might be happening on the ice around the plane. Then we would continue on our way to Esk Lake. We were comfortable with this arrangement because we would still be able to monitor what might develop at Thurston Lake. The pilot clinched the decision by insisting we would have enough time to make a circuit to Esk Lake and return to Thurston prior to any take-off by the plane on the ice. Besides, the pilot down there would have to take heed of the additional aircraft warm-up time required in such cold weather.

The necessary heading to Esk Lake caused us a direction change which blocked our view of Thurston for a few minutes. As soon as we got close enough to verify there was nobody there, we banked towards Thurston once more. As we emerged from the turn, a plane appeared, winging its way straight south and away from us.

"That can't be the plane we saw on the ice, can it?" queried the pilot. "It did not have time to warm up. Either that or they had arrived just before us to take off that quick."

By now, we were close enough to see the ice surface of the entire lake. "Well, there's no plane on the ice now, and that one is the same color as the one we just saw, so it has to be the same one, doesn't it?"

As if on cue, the other plane began to gain altitude and pull away from us. This new development posed its own question. Should we land and check over the area where the plane had landed to see if there were any nets or set lines, or should we try to overtake the plane itself? The fact that no indication of net drag marks were noticed on our first overflight of the site simplified my decision. This was further aided and abetted by the pilot who was giving me the kind of look evident in the eyes of any carnivore when set to strike its prey.

"Well, what do you want to do?" he said, almost champing at the bit.

"I want to know whose plane that is and what they were doing down there" was my reply.

"What kind of government type answer is that? Do you want me to try and catch up with them or not?"

Not wanting to be accused of giving answers to questions in "government lingo", I laughed and said, "do you think we can even catch them?" With that I was thrust back into my seat as the pilot's hand pushed his aircraft to its limits. Only then did he respond to my question.

"Are you kidding?" he laughed. "Unless that sucker has changed his engine from the original factory motor, we don't have a problem. I'll tell you this though, whoever they are, they don't seem to be particularly interested in us catching up to them. I've flown that make of plane many times. It's maxed out right now and we're still gaining on them."

Uh huh, and I could have avoided all of this if I had simply written down the identification number on the plane's wing when we made our first pass. On second thought, that would not have been entirely satisfactory either because I would not have been able to identify the pilot.

We were gaining on them at a high rate of speed. The pilot was in his element, grinning like an over-enthusiastic schoolboy. "I've never been on an official pursuit to catch another plane," he said. "This is fun". He still had that predatory look in his eyes.

Our approach was to the left of the aircraft, and somewhat lower so I could record the I.D. number and check out the identity of the pilot. He turned out to be one of the locals, a fellow who had no previous history of violations with Fish & Wildlife. I could not see who was with him, not that it mattered much now. We turned around and headed back to the lake to take a closer look at what they might have been doing.

Back over Thurston Lake, we circled where the plane had been parked on the ice. There was a hole there large enough to put a net in but no hole to pull it out. There were other signs angling had taken place so we decided to check it all out.

"Can you land a little to the south of where we saw the plane?" I asked the pilot.

"We can have a look, but remember how I like to land near old tracks because I know that if one plane has already landed there, then the chances of us being able to do the same thing are pretty good. We don't really want to hit some concealed overflow that might be deep enough to bury us, do we?" He added the question more in explanation than in the expectation of any reply. So we made a couple of low reconnaissance passes close to the snow-covered ice and that was when we discovered other tracks in the vicinity.

"Yeah. How about let's land over there?" he asked, this time actually waiting for my response. I concurred since it was close to where I wanted to be, yet far enough away from the "evidence" that the prop wash and the skis would not cover any sign of what had been going on.

We got out and walked over to where the plane had been. There were few new tracks, just one where the plane had come in and another where it had taken off again. Close by was the net size hole we had spotted from the air. Also evident was a rectangular imprint in the previous night's skiff of snow, with footprints going to and returning from a number of smaller holes and then leading over to where the plane had been parked. Whatever had made the imprint looked as though it had been picked up by a single individual and put into the plane, at least that was what we surmised. Yet it was strange nonetheless because the ice had not been broken out of any of the holes and the tracks consistently gravitated towards where the plane had been. What on earth had these people been doing? It certainly was not fishing. Since nothing more could be achieved by staying there, we decided to take off for home.

When we arrived back at High Level airport, there at the side of the runway was the plane that we had seen and pursued. The fellow who I had seen flying the aircraft was nowhere to be seen. Nor was there any sign of a box or anything similar that could have made the rectangular imprint in the snow. I thanked my pilot and took my leave, intending to find not so much the "suspect" as the "person of interest".

One major advantage of living in a small place is you know pretty much everybody who lives there. Well, there was his truck parked in his driveway; I had to walk past it to get to his front door. In the back was a large plastic container appearing to be the same size as the imprint in the snow at Thurston Lake. There was no doubt he had seen me drive up because he came out of his house towards me, putting on his jacket as he approached. He was accompanied by some guy I had never seen before. We exchanged greetings then talk about the morning's activities ensued. The plane, it turned out, belonged to his friend, an avid fisherman. So the previous day, they had flown to all the lakes near Bistcho to try their luck. They had taken off and landed so many times at different lakes that they got sloppy and had left their container behind on the ice where it had sat overnight. They missed it when they had arrived back at High Level so a day later, they had flown back to pick it up; just as well, it had in it the walleye limit for two people for one day. The fish had been individually dipped in the lake water many times after death and then frozen as singles to preserve both flesh and flavor. It also made them much easier to count.

Of course I had been recognized when we caught up to them to record their plane's I.D. and to see who was doing the flying. Knowing how active Fish & Wildlife was in the community, they were not in the least surprised I showed up to see what they had been doing. On this particular day, the day when we came across them, they had had no time to fish because the plane's owner had to be home and ready for work on Monday morning; he was one of those types who would never go home without fish no matter what.

Yes, they had licenses, not every investigation ends in high drama!

19 ~ HIDE AND SEEK.

In the late Seventies, I had the pleasure of working on the west end of Lesser Slave Lake for five years. The F & W presence was vitally important. Effective management of a lake that can be fished commercially with nets was crucial to ensure a sustainable fish population; there had to be a reasonable season coupled with a rigorous enforcement program to make it all work.

Information started to trickle into our office of somebody setting small-mesh nets just off the north shore and west of the narrows. This illegal use of nets was a recurring problem for enforcement ever since the criteria for net size and fish quotas was established. Too many fishermen at the time viewed the word criteria as an abstract word that did not apply to whatever they were doing. The size of the mesh on a net is determined first by holding the net up vertically so the mesh forms into a diamond shape. Then, taking the opposing corners of any diamond, you pull them out into a straight line. If you measure the distance between the knots at the ends of the now flattened diamond, you establish mesh size. From there, you correlate that information with the age of the target species of fish to be harvested. This is the most critical step because, as the fishery biologists will tell you, a quarter of an inch up or down in net size can target a different class of fish altogether thereby undermining even the best principles of fish management.

On this occasion, we had a pretty good idea where the nets would be. Our 21 foot stern-drive was gassed up and ready to go. We also decided to take along our 12 car-topper and its nine horse motor for shallower waters. The larger boat was launched with the smaller craft secured crossways on the gunwales just forward of the stern for the nine mile jaunt across the lake to the Narrows. Faust Bay was dead calm but this was no indication as to what the lake itself would be like. As we approached the main body of the lake, a small lively chop was noticeable, but nothing serious. As we proceeded across to the narrows and then west into the open water between the acres of cattails parallel to the shore, there were no nets to be found.

"Jeez, we've come all this way for nothing," griped my partner.

"Hold your horses," I replied. "We must be in the right spot, we have to be! Let me get up on the bow to see if that helps. I should be able to see over the cattails at any rate."

"Okay, but you're probably wasting your time. Take these binoculars, you'll need all the help you can get. Who knows, maybe there are nets in there. Maybe they tied their float lines to sticks or reeds, or who knows what."

The extra two feet or so in height afforded by standing on the bow did in fact allow me to see over the cattails. We had been totally unaware there were large expanses of open water concealed in the middle of these acres and acres of cattails.

"Get up here and take a look at this!" I shouted triumphantly. My companion lumbered his way up to join me on the bow.

"Would you look at that!" he exploded. "There are nets everywhere. The buggers didn't even bother hiding them."

"No kidding," I said shortly, knowing already how much work this was going to be.

My partner was still excited about our find. "See their net floats going off into the cattails? I bet the other end is in the clear water the other side of the cattails so we couldn't see it," he said stating the obvious. "Maybe we've never looked close enough."

Now it was down to business. We unloaded the 12 footer, attached its motor and decided upon a plan of action.

"How about I'll take the small boat out into the open water in the centre of the cattails while you take this boat and snoop around the other cattail beds for more nets."

"Sounds like a plan," my partner replied, eager to get busy.

I got to the first net, followed the floats to an end and began to pull. It was a real strain to get anything to happen. What the hell kind of anchor were they using? Up came a wheel rim off a truck. Very popular among the users of illegal nets, they were easily obtained and very effective on the soft bottom of this lake. Surprisingly, there were some genuine net anchors too. Needless to say, there was no buoy with the customary designated number to mark the end of a legal net. The end of the float line was tied to an anonymous-looking stick, just as my partner had predicted. It was just the kind of illegal setup the poachers knew you would have a hard time seeing. In this case, their plan failed because the floats were showing and because nobody had counted on us taking a look over the top of the cattails.

By now, my partner was off in search of nets between the shore and our current location. I struck out for the open water harboring the net I had first come upon. The net size was three and a half inches; the legal size was five and a half inches when the season was open. Anybody could see that "a blatant violation of the law" such as this could clean out the fish stocks in a number of species very quickly. That's when it struck me that my partner's motor had not been running for very long; at least, I could not hear it. Apparently he too had stopped and was pulling nets. By the sounds of the net floats hitting the side of the boat, he was very busy, and probably as incensed as I was.

For the next four hours or more, we worked steadily picking the fish out of numerous nets. It was a time-consuming and tedious job; we lacked both skill and practice of the commercial fishermen but it had to be done. The net mesh was made with cotton or nylon, not the new monofilament of the day. And since our fish removal skills were so obviously not up to snuff, we found it easier to hold up the fish and to cut the net around it with our finely honed knives. This procedure freed the fish in seconds, though it did not do much for the net! Picking the fish out in the normal fashion would have taken far more time than we had. Besides, one gets a certain satisfaction cutting an illegal net to shreds. Any fish we found still alive were released. By the time we had finished and could not find any more nets, some serious reorganizing had to be done since both boats were haphazardly loaded with fish.

The larger boat contained wooden fish boxes that we used to hold the nets we had not damaged and the fish my partner had retrieved. On the other hand, I had not started out with any boxes. From the front of the centre seat forward to the bow was loaded with fish to the full height of the seat. Any nets we had cut up were piled on top. I had so little freeboard, maybe one or two inches at best, that even the wave created by a fish surfacing could have swamped me.

Traveling dead slow, we made our way to Narrows Creek just west of the Narrows; it was here that the fishermen maintained a stock pile of empty fish boxes supplied by the Fresh Market Fish Corporation. It took us quite a while to get there and to cross the shallows just out from the creek mouth with our heavy loads. On arrival, we boxed fish in the small boat, transferring the full boxes into the larger one. The nets we put into separate boxes. By the time we were finished, the boxes of both fish and nets had consumed every inch of floor space, three boxes deep on the floor, two deep on the seats of the bigger boat. The only parts of the deck that did not carry a box were our front seats and the space in front for our feet. When we had finished, the smaller boat was empty.

We had originally intended to reload the 12 footer the same way as we had when we first crossed the lake. But now given the load already in the larger boat, adding to it the weight of the smaller craft and its motor would have been pushing our luck. Since the water on this day was unusually calm for Lesser Slave Lake, not a even ripple, we decided to run it across under its own power. When you look into Faust Bay from Narrows Creek, you cannot see any buildings you might use as landmarks to guide you across; the skyline south of Faust has to be your guide. You pick the high point of a particular hill, or the slope of a certain valley, and you steer towards it. As long as the weather cooperates, by the time you are halfway across, you will be able to spot the buildings leading you to the dock and the launch area.

"Moccasin telegraph" is a mystical phenomenon that can leave you totally baffled. It is a form of communication where information about something you were doing reaches your destination before you do, this in an era and a location where there is definitively no modern technology to accomplish the task. So, as we approached the dock, there was an unusual number of people and vehicles. As we tied up, the inevitable questions began.

"Holy! Where did you get all them fish?"(As if you didn't know!)

"Who caught them all, you guys?"(Who else do you suppose?)

"That's one heck of a load for a small boat like that. Aren't you grossly overloaded?"(What do you care?)

"Are you gonna sell those nets?" (You wish!)

"Say, I wouldn't mind buying the anchors."(Dream on! I have no intention of pulling them out one more time!)

"What are you going to do with the fish, sell 'em to the mink ranch?"

"Did you guys get them at the Narrows?"

That last question stopped us in our tracks. We stopped transferring fish from our boat to our truck and looked knowingly at each other. Both of us then made a beeline for the man and escorted him to a spot where nobody else could hear what was being said.

"And why would you suppose that we got them at the Narrows?" I asked. But this fellow was too quick for us this day.

"Oh, I heard some of the guys saying they were going to the Narrows. Damn, who was it now? No, no, for the life of me I can't remember."

Oh well, we had made our point. It was time to let him go and for us to finish our chore.

We loaded everything and set off for the fish plant, properly called "The Fresh Water Market Fish Corporation", to whom all commercially caught fish had to be sold by law. "Our catch" was sold with the proceeds going to the provincial government. Believe it or not, our haul was close to 1,500 pounds. As for the floats and the lead weights from the nets, they went to the local biologist for use on his nets. What remained of the other nets was burned. At least our little foray would slow down the illegal fishermen until they found some new gear for themselves. And now the cover was blown when it came to the cattails!

20 ~ HIBERNATION BLUES.

The trials and tribulations of the North American black bear are legendary for all those who have had occasion to deal with them in their line of work or to chase them away from their field or campsite. The bears usually causing most of the problems for humans are the two, three, and four year olds. Generally speaking, by the time they have made it to four, they have undergone some behavior modification courses from their peers, or from people, to instill more acceptable behavior and to improve their chances of survival in a particular area. Sometimes, whatever behavior modification has taken place is in turn overpowered by one of two things, instinct or indolence. We have all heard those black bear stories where bears steal people's food, tear down their tents, wreak havoc with their beehives, that sort of thing, but what about a bear taking up residence in a culvert?

High Prairie late in the fall, with barely a dusting of snow on the ground, just enough to do some rudimentary tracking if the need arose. The phone rang; it was the local highway maintenance foreman.

"Hi! You're gonna love this one! There's a very large bear getting ready to hibernate in one of our culverts just east of town. It's been seen taking arm loads of hay into the culvert a number of times already. Now if some damn fool shoots it in there in the spring, the runoff of water will be blocked and we'll end up with a major flood on our hands. So is there some way you guys can get it out for us?"

"Aren't you just the bearer of great news?" I responded somewhat sarcastically, still not entirely convinced the man was serious. "A live bear in a culvert, ready to hibernate, eh? With hibernation coming on, it could be a bit lethargic, but you want me to be the guy crazy enough to crawl in and find out. I guess none of your guys would do it, that's why you phoned us?"

"Well, I have to say that I was as suspicious as you are right now. We were told about it just yesterday so a couple of us drove out there to see if it was true. The tracks tell me that there is definitely something there, and that it is very big."

"Well, are you certain that it is a bear that is there?" I asked skeptically. "I mean, nobody that I know of has ever heard of a bear hibernating in a culvert."

"Oh, he's there all right, he's there. There were all sorts of bear tracks going in and out of the culvert. And you know that there was a dusting of snow last night? Well there were fresh tracks in the snow this morning. So we took a flashlight and shone it in at both ends. All you can see is hay, it's solid in there, almost to both ends of the culvert. There's no way we want that bear to die in there because it will stop the flow of water in spring when the snow melts and you know what a mess that will make, don't you? There'll be a hell of a mess. You've gotta get it out for us."

"Okay, okay," I said. "But it's almost dark right now so we'll go out tomorrow at sunup and take a look. It sounds like an exercise that will require daylight. From what you have said, it doesn't sound as though the bear is going any place anyway, right?"

"Right," agreed the voice on the other end of the line. "And that'll be great if you can do it. By the way, if you do need any help, give me a call." I thanked him mentally for the offer, but I well knew any help you acquired in such circumstances had to be experienced help, otherwise the level of danger tended to increase unacceptably.

The next morning saw us on our way east out of town. "So, just how are we going to get that darn bear out of there?" I asked my partner, mainly out of curiosity.

"You know, I gave that a great deal of thought last night and could not come up with any solution that sounded at all reasonable," was his contribution. "I am relying on your wisdom and experience," he added smugly, and I thought somewhat sarcastically.

"Well, we can stop at the warehouse and take a look-see if there is anything that we might be able to use to help us. But we had better check out the situation first, before we do anything. I couldn't find anything at home this morning that would be any help at all."

"This should be the culvert coming up," my partner, who was also doubling as the navigator, interrupted me. We stopped on the road above it and looked down.

"Yeah, there's hay at this end of it with some snow on it. I can't see any sign of fresh tracks though."

"Let me move ahead and turn around. Then we can walk back and take a closer look."

"Hold on. I'll get out first and check things out while you are turning around," said my intrepid colleague. He hopped out while I made a U-turn further down the road and stopped twenty yards or so short of the culvert. I also made a point of leaving both truck doors open in the event we needed sudden refuge. It was then we considered what options we might have. We talked about using long poles to poke the bear and make him come out. Bad idea, we said; neither of us felt like trying to outrun an angry bear intent on chomping on some ne'er-do-well foolish enough to disturb his slumber. Okay, then how about we flood it out? Bad idea, we said; we had no pump and no running water to pump in anyway. Okay, let's shoot through the culvert with a high powered rifle. We would then wait an hour and then start cleaning out the hay. Of course, all of this was based on the assumption that we would come upon a dead bear. All we would have to do is pull out the carcass. Bad idea; what if the hay absorbed all of the energy of the bullet before it struck the bear? We would end up with one very live and very cantankerous bear on our hands. Not good.

"The pencil flares! What about the pencil flares? We could shoot them into the hay at each end of the culvert, they will set the hay on fire, and the bear will come out." My partner, always on the ball, was jubilant.

"Yeah, that should work," I replied hesitantly, still not convinced that fire and bear would necessarily make a good mix. Nevertheless, the idea sent us on a hunt through the toolbox for the launcher and the flares. Finally, we came up with six flares and, wonder of all wonders, we even found the launcher. When eventually we were ready to do battle, one of us was armed with flares, the other with the standard issue shotgun. My partner shot a flare into each end of the culvert and then we stood back and waited. Thick white smoke started to billow out of the bear's new home.

"We'll get some action now for sure," commented my colleague excitedly.

"Maybe, maybe not," I said, putting a damper on his enthusiasm. "Take a look at the far end. It has quit smoking entirely." Somehow the flares had simply petered out. There was only one thing left to do, load up and try again. We repeated the previous routine, only this time firing two flares into one end and one into the other. Again we waited, and waited some more. There did not appear to be much smoke nor any fire this time, so we contemplated a quick trip back to town to pick up some more flares. One thing a Fish and Wildlife officer is good at is waiting. Patience is less a virtue and more of an inevitability in our line of work. We waited a bit longer. The occasional puff of smoke wafted out of the opening to dissipate lazily into thin air. Suddenly, sporadic billows of smoke began to appear; something must have moved in the culvert giving the smoldering hay inside some much-needed oxygen, which in turn created just enough combustion to generate more smoke. On the other hand, there was little danger the hay would become a roaring inferno because it was damp and there was clearly not enough oxygen. So there we were, grey day, light snow now falling, low clouds, and our visibility reduced by the smoke coming from the smoldering hay. Both openings were now blowing smoke with some zest.

"I hope that bear does come out, we don't want the bugger asphyxiated in there, do we? That'll defeat our whole purpose of trying to give it another chance before we have to resort to other measures." I was still concerned the boys on the road maintenance crew might try and do it themselves if we failed. The last thing we all needed was uninitiated do-gooders fooling around with bears, somebody could get themselves hurt, or worse still, killed.

"We've got lots of time," responded my partner. "The bear is probably only now getting the message. Smoke is a great bear motivator and it's sure smoking now."

"At least we won't have to drive into town for more flares," I said.

More waiting, more watching, adrenalin going to waste. The smoke thickened up even more making it almost impenetrable. The culvert opening twenty yards away was barely discernible. Suddenly in the billowing mantle of gray and white, a menacing black silhouette slowly appeared, looking first one way and then the other. Whether it was the smoke back grounded by the snow, or whether it was simply our own anticipation making that bear look larger than life, we shall never know. It was massive, gigantic. How it had ever fit itself into a culvert in the first place, I have no idea. He stopped and checked us out. Out of the corner of my eye, I glimpsed my partner's shotgun making its way silently up to his shoulder. I knew however, he would never shoot without much more in the way of naked aggression on the part of the bear. As if checking for traffic, the bear looked both ways again before nonchalantly ambling off into the bush.

As the shotgun came down, my partner echoed my observation. "Was it me, or did that bear seem mighty big to you?"

"You bet," I said. "Let's go take a look at his tracks." They turned out to be bigger than usual, but not exceptional.

"Well I sure hope he has time to find a better spot to den before winter turns too cold. I hope too that bears care if their den has smoke damage. We don't need that big boy coming back!"

"Ah, you're too much of a pessimist. Be an optimist instead. We'll go back and phone the highways crew and let them know that their bear has left town on a one-way ticket. They may as well come back and deal with the fire in the culvert."

That was the last we saw or heard of that bear. We can only hope it did well and its choice of habitation was a little less highbrow.

21 ~ SCALPED

It's another world, up there in the land of the midnight sun. Things happen that are truly stranger than fiction. A phone call from the police at four in the morning; some hapless fellow has been scalped by a bear.........oh, but I'm getting ahead of myself.

The day begins with the call. A short time later, a police car rolls into the yard; they need my help. I jump in and while the driver is doing a very remarkable job of avoiding the potholes on the Mackenzie Highway at just shy of warp speed, I find myself reflecting they must undergo rigorous training. During the next 25 minutes of zinging and zagging, a bizarre story unfolds.

A native man has been helped into the Meander River ranger station with his entire scalp torn loose by a bear. The forest officer on duty is faced with only one choice in the circumstances; he helps the man into his truck and is now en route to the health nurse in High Level to get treatment for his passenger. This means we will meet him somewhere on the highway so he can brief us about the situation. It is our responsibility to ensure for reasons of public safety there is not some bear roaming around out there with an extreme hate for humanity. Okay, at least we know what to look for, a green Forestry Truck. That should be no problem seeing the traffic on the highway is so sparse at this time of day.

Here comes a truck now! It's green, yup, it's a Forestry Truck. It's got to be him! Sure enough. We stop. The cop talks to the forestry officer. I just have to get out and see what happened. There's no way it can be as bad as they had made it out to be. As I round the front of the forestry truck, I see a diminutive figure hunched over on the passenger side, a gray blanket covering everything from his eyes upwards. As I get closer, a vivid red and very fresh-looking wound is evident below the blanket. It starts from just above the right eyebrow and makes its way on to the visible part of the eyelid, sinks down into the cheek and continues to the bottom of the jaw line. A moment of thoughtless curiosity motivates the question.

"What else happened?" I regret that question as soon as it is out of my mouth.

The man is unperturbed. Slowly, ever so slowly, he begins removing the blanket from his head. As he carefully folds it back ,the gash continues on into the hairline. When the blanket is pulled just past his ears, the whole scalp begins to move. Now he has the attention of all of us. As he moves the blanket even further back, the scalp itself begins to slide sideways, the whole scalp from somewhere above the left ear around the front of his head just back of the hair line to with in an inch of the top of his right ear continuing around to the back of his head falls to the left side of his head. The only thing keeping the scalp from completely falling off are a couple of inches of in tact skin above and back of the left ear. A kind of white membrane replete with tiny pulsating blood vessels covers an all too visible skull. Very calmly, he reaches up with his left hand and readjusts it back on to his head as if he is replacing an errant hairpiece. That single move leaves us in total awe. How can he be so calm, so detached? Must be shock. Then he proceeds to fold the blanket back into its original position. Without so much as a word being said, all three of us are witness to something that we will never forget, a sight that we all hope we will never see again.

All the Forestry Officer is able to tell us is some guy in a pickup had shot the bear after the attack and that it was last seen up the road in the ditch some 200 yards from where the attack took place.

"I'd better get moving now," he adds. "Don't want to miss that nurse, not with this guy like he is."

We continue on our way arriving at the attack site within the hour. Here we get the full story from another Forestry Officer. It seems the native was bringing a saddle horse from Paddle Prairie to Meander River. The shortest route to follow was afforded by the Mackenzie Highway. The man had been riding in the ditch and on the back slope of the highway for three days straight. Exhausted, even though he was only seven or so miles from home, he decided to stop and rest. We could only surmise this was when he was attacked by the bear. Obviously he could not tell us. Immediately after the attack, he was apparently in such shock that he was unable to tell anyone what had transpired.

However, we are able to piece together something of the incident with the information the rescuers had given to the forest officer. An 18 wheeler on its way north is passing a clump of trees. Suddenly, on the back slope of the highway, the driver and his companion see a bear dragging what looked like a rag doll off into the bush, its head firmly in the bear's mouth. Without giving it a second thought, they skid to a stop spraying gravel everywhere. Out of the cab they jump, screaming and yelling at the top of their lungs and running towards the bear, throwing sticks and stones at it as they go. Unnerved by all this commotion, the bear lets go of his meal and heads for the safety of the bush. The man he was dragging lies where he dropped, completely inert. One of the truckers scoops him gently up into his arms and they turn back towards the truck. That's the moment when the second trucker looks behind him. At the same instant as he hears a hair-raising growl, he sees the bear not six steps behind him, determined to recapture his meal. Luckily, still in his hand he is carrying a fair-sized rock which he immediately lobs at the bear. Thank God! The bear is distracted enough that they make it to the edge of the road where there is a guardrail. As he runs, the unburdened man picks up more rocks and sticks. Just as well. The bear decides to take another run at them. As the first trucker yanks open the cab door and bundles the injured man inside, the second is pelting the bear with a barrage of sticks and stones. As the bear nears the guardrail, it is the clang of stones on metal that finally unsettles him, hopefully for good. This gives his newly intended target time to clamber into the truck beside the others.

At this point, a pickup appears going in the other direction. The driver actually sees the last part of the rescue and decides to get into the action. He grabs the big game rifle he is carrying in his truck and fires at the bear as it is heading back to the bush. You guessed it! He misses at 40 yards and the bear disappears. Everybody's attention now turns to the critically injured man; that's when the decision is made to transfer him to the pickup and take him to the Forestry Office at Meander River. While all this business is going on, low and behold, a bear appears some 200 yards further up the road. Not to be outdone this time, same guy, same gun, bang! The bear is dead. Misses at 40, kills at 200, go figure!

We locate the dead bear and remove the head so we can send it off for a rabies check. Oh sure, nobody could ever say positively this was the same bear. However, according to all of the witnesses, this one looked to be the same size and color as the one encountered dragging the unfortunate victim into the bush. Further investigation turns up the ball cap that the scalped man was wearing. It has four distinct holes in it, two on each side representing the bears upper and lower incisors. There can be no doubt that these were made by the bear's incisors, the very same that tore off the victim's scalp. With the gobs of bear saliva on the crown of the cap, you have all the evidence you need that this bear had a great appetite and had intended to make a meal out of his sleeping find.

The Forest Officer duly delivered the wounded man to the nurse at High Level. She did a thorough assessment, cleaned his wounds up as best she could, administered some pain killers, and had him flown off to Edmonton for further repair. As she recounted later, she found claw marks on the left side of the body but they were not severe. Surprisingly too, there were no broken bones, no life-threatening injuries as such beyond the scalp.

Time to skip ahead four months. Only now can we piece together the rest of the story. I interview our survivor using an interpreter. Here is what was learned.

The native man and his horse were almost home but the man decided both of them were so fatigued they needed a rest. He dismounted, removed the saddle and bridle, and tied his horse up to a bush. Now desperate for a bit of shuteye, he took out the horse blanket, rolled himself up in it, and within seconds was fast asleep. The next thing to register on his mind was a bizarre kind of scratching going on above and around his feet. Still half asleep and reluctant yet to come to life, he kicked out at whatever was doing the scratching. It did not work, so he lashed out again. The scratching persisted, so he sat up to find out what it was that would not leave him alone. The instant he raised his head and saw it was a bear scratching at his legs, the bear clamped his jaws around his skull. He was literally yanked out of his blanket and was being dragged off into the thickest brush about 20 feet away when the 18 wheeler burst in on the scene. You know all about the rescue.

I cannot say how long the victim spent in hospital as I did not come across him for quite some time after his return home. When eventually we did come face to face, he looked exactly how I remembered him prior to the bear attack, the only difference being a drooping eyelid caused by some muscle damage by tooth or claw. Of course, there were other injuries not so visible. Until the day he was attacked, he used to spend a good deal of his time trapping on his own. Not any more. From that day on, he always made sure he was accompanied by someone else.

All in all, there was a positive outcome to this story. The native trapper got to retain his scalp with the added bonus of a full head of hair. A potentially dangerous bear was taken out of circulation, and what's more, it proved not to have rabies. As for the horse, I never inquired, but to this day I am curious as to why it never snorted and pawed at the ground, waking up its owner when the bear was skulking around.

22 ~ RABBITS. NO REALLY!

The call from a neighboring district officer started things going. He had been receiving a stream of information of some beaver trapping going on along the road to Carcajou, east of Keg River, by folks with no business being there. So he and I arranged to meet at the Keg River ranger station late one afternoon in the spring of 1968. Meeting here afforded me a place to leave my patrol vehicle and for us to discuss whatever new developments had occurred. It so happened there were new developments. A description of the vehicle and the number of times the person had gone out to poach beavers on somebody else's trap line had been phoned in, and not just once either. Of course, in small communities or sparsely settled areas, everybody knows everybody else's business. And you could bet your bottom dollar if we did not respond to the complaints in a timely fashion, then somebody might not think twice about taking the law into his own hands with potentially disastrous consequences. When we were given the fellow's name, we knew he had to be a poacher because all the trap lines and the people who work them are registered at a Fish and Wildlife Office. He was not registered anywhere.

A short drive in the officer's unmarked car put us on the road to Carcajou. A long, straight road, it ran to about 20 miles of gravel, no bends, no turns, all the way to Carcajou. For the most part, it travels through good beaver country, full of permanent sloughs and interconnecting creeks, a beaver paradise. There was an abundance of the beaver's favorite dish, trembling aspen more commonly referred to as poplar. Acres of willows were also growing both in and out of the water. Many of these were harvested by the beaver to weave into their houses and their dams, along with a blend of mud and rocks making them almost impenetrable. We drove across the first creek that we came upon, seeking out a vantage point that would give us a clear view for miles. Out came the binoculars.

What appeared to be an old truck was parked about a mile away facing in the direction we were going. We needed to make a decision, stay put to see if someone was to come out of the bush carrying a beaver, trapping equipment, a rifle, whatever, or move in and make the best of what we found there. The truck certainly seemed to match the description phoned in to us but we were unable to make out the exact colors because it was so dirty. Besides, it was now starting to rain. After a lengthy discussion, we decided to drive by and give ourselves a closer look, we did have an unmarked car after all. We knew if we stayed where we were, we could easily have ended up watching an abandoned vehicle; on the other hand, our drive-by could blow the whole thing if the suspect came ambling out of the bush just as we got there. Or else, if he spotted us from in the bush, he could easily drop whatever he was carrying and deny any knowledge about anything connected to beavers. We moseyed along slowly as if we were a couple of old-timers looking for an easy beaver to poach. The distance to the truck turned out to be just over a mile, and yes, it was the truck we were looking for. We took a big gamble because we needed to have some idea of how long the truck had been parked there.

Coming up to the truck, we spotted at once the fresh tracks going off the gravel and into the soft dirt on the edge of the road. Inside the vehicle, yet quite visible, we saw extra shells, some clothes and some boots. The hood of the vehicle was a little warmer than the rest of the truck so it could not have been parked there long ago. We would have liked to have investigated further but, given how warm the hood was, and given the light rain and the fact the sun had just gone down, our man was likely not far away. It was better for us to take up our original position and see what happened next. Wouldn't you know it, the rain increased, partially obscuring our view, but also hopefully obscuring us from our subject. Moving the car to a better position at this moment would surely have tipped him off so we hunkered down and waited. The quiet was almost surreal, as if Nature herself was holding her breath too. Out came the trusty binoculars again; at least they helped a little and gave us the illusion we were actually doing something. Being a dead-end road , one consolation to us was the suspect would have to pass us to get to the main highway.

Waiting, and more waiting. "What the hell, let's have a bite to eat", suggested my companion. Out came the food, the sandwiches and the thermos. Both of us knew Murphy's Law would come into play, as soon as we were at our most inconvenient, something would happen. It didn't. Murphy must have been out of town that day. We ate all we had, even put away the containers and whatnot just as our mothers had taught us, and still nothing happened. Moreover, the daylight was clearly beginning to fade.

"There he is!" blurted out my partner. "There he is. There's somebody on the road behind the truck. He's walking towards it."

Our binoculars quickly picked up a man with a rifle in one hand, a beaver in the other. Immediately, we set off in the car, hoping to catch him outside his truck avoiding a chase. The air was very still and, even though we were about a mile away, the man spun around and looked towards us when our car came to life. But then he turned away and continued on towards his vehicle, although we could not see just how close he was to it. He was coming up the tailgate of his truck as we approached. We noticed his right shoulder drop momentarily and then straighten up as he took a couple of steps forward to face us. The beaver had vanished. An inkling of things not being quite right, somehow not being quite what they seemed, must have struck him. Certainly the unmarked car had served our purpose admirably. I was sure the beaver could not have been thrown into the ditch nor into the bush. That left only one place, under the truck, but neither of us could see it. We had stopped just behind the truck but in the center of the road. Not disappointed in the least, we went into our act; my partner's task was to divert the suspect's attention, talking about things of common interest, while I would surreptitiously take a look around the suspect vehicle. My partner was doing such a great job, the man never even saw me get down on my hands and knees to look under his truck. Boy, that man had to have some throwing arm! There was the beaver lying eight or so feet from the back of the box under the truck. All this time, I could hear my partner chatting innocently with the suspect, enquiring about what he had been doing, telling him we had seen him coming out of the bush and were wondering why a man would be coming out of the bush alone.

"Yes, I was in the bush," said the man smoothly. "Me and my buddy are partners on a trap line. It was my turn to check it out today."

"Oh really," returned my colleague. "Then how come your name is not on file for this particular trap line?"

Oh, he was a quick one, this fellow! He did not miss a beat. "Oh, that's because we did all our paperwork at High Level." I was on the point of crawling under the truck to retrieve the beaver when I heard this.

I straightened up and said, "I don't think so. You see, unfortunately for you, I'm the guy that runs the Fish and Wildlife Office in High Level and there have been no partnerships registered there for this trap line."

Incredibly, the man was still unfazed. "Well, it probably doesn't matter much because I was actually out hunting rabbits."

"Oh, so you were not hunting beaver at all then?" asked my partner.

"No. I was hunting rabbits. I'm not into hunting beaver with a rifle. It's one hell of a lot easier to trap 'em," he said smugly.

As do all pairs of investigators working together, my partner had expertly maneuvered the suspect into turning his back on my activities. His timing was perfect. I hauled out the beaver and stood up, holding it up by the tail. That's when my colleague suggested the suspect turn around.

There I was, grinning away, the beaver held high. This elicited a stream of diatribe having absolutely no effect on his audience. But he was quick, this fellow, as we already knew. All at once, his story turned into one of poverty and starvation.

"Go easy on me, guys. I haven't had a job all winter. The beaver is to feed my wife and kids." Ah, but we had been around too long to fall for that one. We exchanged knowing looks. The man was wearing new rubber boots, and a pretty decent-looking jacket and pants did not indicate great poverty to us. His sudden switch from partner on a trap line to rabbit hunter on the verge of destitution had been accomplished with seamless ease. What would be his next tack? But it was my partner's call, it was his district. Like me, he bought none of it. The ticket was written, the rifle and the beaver were seized, and the court date was set. Not to be seen as too callous, and with a huge generosity of spirit, my colleague told the suspect we would be happy to investigate the circumstances regarding his claim to poverty and we would communicate with him further depending on what we found out. For once the man had nothing to say!

Three days later, I was back in the office doing the interminable paperwork thing when the phone rang. It was my colleague calling back about our recent dealings with the beaver hunter on the road to Carcajou. "So what did you find out?" I asked.

After a colorful diatribe about the man's ancestry, my partner explained that the fellow had been working on an oil rig all winter and had just come home, so he had money, and plenty of it. We would let the judge decide was our unanimous opinion.

It seemed that when the judge did get the story from both sides, his genial appearance belied his mood. The accused was found guilty. The sentencing was the interesting part. The judge mentioned the man's attempts to mislead the investigators. In his view, such attempts were just as serious as the misdemeanor itself, hence the sentence. Forfeiture of the firearm to the Crown, forfeiture of the beaver, and a fine three times the normal minimum fine. He would not be hunting beavers legally or illegally for a while, of that we were quite certain!

23 ~ I'M NOT JOKING DEAR, NOT THIS TIME

It has to be said, sometimes one should not be too quick at taking people up on offers they might make, especially where it involves an airplane taking off and landing with a stranger at the controls. Having said that, during a period of sparse operating budgets and in ones eagerness to do things better, caution may be thrown to the winds. Of course, the smooth reassurance of the pilot's thousands of hours of flying time in all types of aircraft over a span of 20 years helps to allay any additional qualms in the matter. The upshot is - a deal is made. I will supply the fuel. After lunch, we head for the airfield, ready for our three hour trip.

When I saw what we were actually going up in, my heart skipped a few beats. Single engine I expected, but canvas-covered? "Don't they make them out of metal now?" I thought to myself. And the side-by-side seating gave me the uncomfortable sense of being crammed into a two seater coffin with the lid open. In the interests of diplomacy, I keep my dark thoughts to myself. The tanks are filled, final checks are completed, here we are, taxiing down the runway on a perfect day for flying. Okay, I console myself, the strip seems a little rough but nothing that a composition of rubber, canvas, and the odd piece of light metal cannot handle. However, there are two oddities I had not expected. The first of these was the dual controls. Not too big a deal; "thou shalt not touch," I lecture myself sternly. "Not in any circumstances." The second was the word "HANDLE" painted in big letters on the door above the handle. This was different, a bit stark if I may say so. Oh well, it must be there to assist you if you should get too disoriented and want to climb out in mid-flight.

We're off the ground, gaining altitude and heading west. So far, so good. My pilot points out a dark gray band of cloud of undetermined thickness crossing the sky at right angles to our general direction. According to him, it is a line of demarcation between a high pressure and a low pressure area.

"Is that right?" I comment, wondering if he is trying to convince me he is wise in the ways of the weather. Certainly for me, it comes across as a useless piece of information.

We fly on, northwest towards McLennan, over a patchwork of farmland, bush and sloughs. As we cruise along, the pilot is happily pointing out places where he had landed previously with his wife on their customary Sunday picnics. Again I have to wonder; is he telling me all this to pacify my nerves, especially as he knows I want to land in a pasture to investigate a complaint of wolves killing cattle? Whatever the reason, he inspires me with confidence. Our flight turns to the south-east, taking us in sight of Buffalo Bay and Lesser Slave Lake. There is not a ripple to be seen, the few boats and birds appearing as black and white dots on a lake of pristine blue. No excitement here! We change direction towards the south, crossing the lake near Joussard.

It's time now to match map to terrain to pinpoint the location of the wolf/cattle problem. It takes a few minutes but soon we are on to it. There's a shack, a small lake, and a road all where our hand-drawn map indicates that they are supposed to be.

"Don't you worry about that, the pasture is big enough to land any small plane on," the map's author had pronounced with great authority. After the first over flight, the pilot apparently agrees. But wait! From our 1,500 foot vantage point, the gray irregular blobs scattered haphazardly in the pasture look a little too much like rocks to my way of thinking, and what's more, they are situated in such a way they would preclude any thought of landing in between them. We nose our way down to take a closer look. Ah, at 200 feet, we see not rocks but mature seasoned cow-pies. One other thing; at midfield there is a vehicle trail worn into the ground six to eight inches deep, the trail leading off to the shack.

"Not to worry," says my pilot blithely. "We don't need that much field. We'll be stopped well before we get to that." Okay, he knows what he is doing, he's landed in lots of fields before with his wife on their Sunday outings.

"Go for it!" I say unwittingly.

We circle round to line up for the landing. No wind, no trees as we approach the fence line from the north. Aren't we a little high for the length of the pasture? Not a good time to voice my amateurish questions, so I button my lip. We touch down. 'Er, that was touched down, because now we're up in the air again. Did we really hit that hard? Nah, must be those fat tires he's got. Down we go a second time. Bang, crash, then back up again. Oh damit! That trail seems to be getting very close in a big big hurry.......and if these bounces continue on the way they are, we could hit it and flip, couldn't we? Down once more, only this time we suddenly cease all forward progress and start flipping over forwards, all in a sort of surreal slow motion. I see the sky, I see the trees, I see the ground, the roof, the interior of the cockpit , all spinning by in a strange kaleidoscope of images. And now here I am, hanging upside down, suspended only by my seat belt. I tip my head and peer out of the windshield. Oh no! Gas is dripping steadily to the ground from the gas tank mounted above the motor, not my idea of safe at all. What if some hot piece falls off the motor into the growing puddle of gas beneath? This thought inspires me to leave A.S.A.P. , right this second. Where's the darn door handle for Pete's sake? Oh.....so that's why the word "HANDLE" is painted so boldly on the door! Some astute fellow must have known one day I might find myself hanging upside down in somebody's cow-pied pasture looking for the door handle. I open the door ready to clamber out. Now what the hell is going on, asks my befuddled brain. I cannot move. Oh, but of course, the seat belt is still fastened. Panic not! I push myself back up to relieve pressure on the belt.

"Success! Success! I did it!" I want to tell the world as I scrape my hands and knees on the roof below me. This is bright, crawling out of an open door on the underside of the wing. I stand up and take a couple of very tentative steps. "Damn! Where is the pilot? What the hell has happened to my pilot?"

Back down on my hands and knees. There he is, still upside down, and still fighting a great fight with his seat belt. I am halfway through the door when his seat belt lets go, depositing him on the roof in an undignified heap. To my surprise, he exits though my door instead of his. He's disoriented no doubt.

What do you know, all is well with us humans, but the plane, oh the plane, it resembles something out of a cartoon. It looks, well, forlorn flipped upside down like that. The prop is folded back neatly, almost touching the edge of the circle of fuel-soaked grass, that is clearly undecided as to whether to catch fire or not. The tail is bent over sideways, about a third of the way down. The whole mess just sits there like some gigantic wounded bird.

Now a new phenomenon begins; people start arriving from who knows where. It's as if we had kicked over an ant nest. While we had been up in the air searching for the right location and lining up to land, we saw no sign neither of people nor their vehicles. First one, then three, then five; to the best of my recollection, ten or twelve vehicles showed up within the first 15 minutes, all accommodating more than one passenger.

I found this whole business very difficult to understand, especially considering the crash took place below the height of the surrounding trees. Add to this the fact, on our approach, there was no evidence of human habitation, except of course for the deserted shack on the one side of the deserted pasture. Moreover, we were at the end of a dead-end road. You have to bear in mind this all took place in the pre-cell phone era. You figure it out! All of them, without exception, wanted to know how we were; very considerate but it got a bit tedious repeating the story over and over.

Talk turns to plane damage, the pilot's only concern being how he could get it back to his hangar in High Prairie. We persuade one of our audience to give us a ride to town and on the way we discuss the logistics of transporting the aircraft back to base. Fish and Wildlife comes to the rescue once again. After supper, we would meet at the Fish and Wildlife warehouse and unload the 21 foot boat and requisition its trailer to haul the battered fuselage home. The wings we would take off and throw into the back of a half ton. Everything is arranged by the time we reach the airport and retrieve our trucks for the ride home to supper.

I come into the house at the usual time and in the usual manner. I go into the kitchen where my wife is working at the sink facing the window. Out came the usual "how was your day, dear? How was your plane ride?"

"We crashed," was all I could say.

A pregnant silence as the news sank in. "You what?" she turns slowly, a look between the emotions of horror and relief etched across her face. She knows as soon as she sees me that I am not joking, not this time. She sits down unsteadily at the kitchen table.

"Tell me about it" she asks almost breathlessly.

24 ~ FOLLOW THOSE BUBBLES

It is not often something as fleeting as a string of bubbles lasts long enough to be enjoyed for anything beyond its immediate beauty. Naturally, water and bubbles go together; on this occasion, they offered up an intriguing mystery.

It was at a spot between Buffalo Bay and Lesser Slave Lake where a water course connected both bodies of water. Here, there was a bridge that led to the only sheltered boat launch allowing access without having to contend with the wind. Both the canal and the larger expanses of water boasted one of the most prolific walleye populations of a good size for both anglers and commercial fishermen. This gave rise to two scenarios, a huge increase in the number of anglers in the late spring when the run was on, and a surge in the number of illegal nets because there was always a market for walleye. So it behooved Fish and Wildlife Officers to do their best to monitor both fisheries to keep some semblance of order.

Just prior to sunup on a morning in June, I was launching my 16 foot runabout with its 75 h.p. outboard motor, a good size for the early Seventies for something purchased by the government. At the time, some of the resident commercial fishermen left their boats at this launching site. I happened to notice that one of them was not there but did not think too much about it at the time; he could have gone to another lake for all I knew. I completed my launch, tied up my boat, and parked my truck and trailer out of the way. It seemed somehow strange there were no boats out nor anglers on the bridge, but perhaps everybody had decided to sleep in this particular day. Regardless, it was time for an early morning ride to check things out; it could very well be somebody had accessed the water from somewhere else and was now out on the lake. A check for nets would do no harm. I got turned around and started down the canal towards the lake. I never saw it this calm, not a ripple anywhere. The only sign of life on the water was a group of Western Grebes and an assortment of ducks. That was when I noticed two distinct parallel lines of bubbles about four feet apart, going in the same direction as I was, and continuing straight on out of sight.

To anyone who has spent much time in the great outdoors, the very notion of a straight line of any length is unusual, two parallel lines this long was nothing short of extraordinary. They certainly captured my imagination; surely they could only have been made by some form of human activity, but what? The bubbles were about the size of a quarter and there were myriads of them in each line. My hope was the wind would not suddenly get up and erase them. There was less and less doubt in my mind that they had been produced by some kind of motorboat. If the wind did decide to make it's presence known, and with so great an expanse of open water with acres of cat tails to hide among, there would be no chance of finding the boat, not that there was any indication of illegal activity at this point despite my suspicions.

I traveled about a mile down the channel from the bridge to the west end of the lake proper. In the distance, I could see a slight ripple on the water. Although it had not yet reached my location, I lost my line of bubbles. I stood up on the back of the boat seat to take a last scan of the area through my binoculars. Bingo! There was what looked to be a line of bubbles some distance over to the north-east. Yes, yes that was it, but it was distorting fast. Okay, it had maintained a north-east direction so I would carry on and see where it led. Eventually the bubbles simply disappeared, telling me there had to be a boat somewhere nearby. I was astounded how far it was to the shore through the cat tails, and how tall they were. If someone was hiding among them, somehow I would have to raise myself high enough that I could look down on them rather than over them. This called for the antics of a contortionist. With the boat barely moving. I put one foot down on the back of the seat, the other on the dashboard, and a paddle blade held to the floor to help me balance. Great! Now I could see pretty well......but I could not reach the steering wheel. A modification of my strategy was necessary based on the premise that I had to have height to see into those cat tails. I realigned myself along the edge of the growth and resumed my position up on my precarious perch. The steering would not be critical related to speed, but at least I would be able to go straight for some distance. Hello, what was this? More bubbles, not many, but the right configuration nonetheless. They also looked the same in size but the wind had stirred them up a bit so I could not be certain. Still nothing. Then a plethora of bubbles right at the edge of a heavy clump of cat tails, and some of the cat tails did not look quite right......

I admit now I must have presented a peculiar picture in my own right, perched precariously over a paddle and straining to see into the morass of vegetation. Again, nothing. I drifted on, like a one-legged heron, my hopes beginning to fade.

What! Why were those cat tails leaning sideways in the shape of a V? The V merged into a patch of taller cat tails. And now the color red where everything was supposed to be green and brown? It was a boat, and not an abandoned one either. By now I had drifted parallel to it and could see directly down into the cat tail patch. There, making himself as small as possible, was one of the area's long-time residents and a commercial fisherman. It was undeniably comical. He sat there, drawn up like a beaver on the seat and deck of his boat and looking every bit like an old tarp, except for that shiny face and those defiant eyes. The latter were averted to one side, probably in the forlorn hope that I would not see him. Soon I was surveying the entire length of his boat from stem to stern; there was no sign of a net, nor of any other fishing gear for that matter. But there was a weather-beaten tarp covering a large mound of something in the center of the boat.

Bill and I went way back. He had been ticketed for several previous fishing violations, and depending what was under that tarp, he was about to get another one. The sporadic combinations of four letter words coming from his mouth, unprintable in anybody's book, seemed to presuppose his guilt. The diatribe included castigations of himself for being so dumb to let a fish cop catch him again and naturally he castigated me for being the one to catch him again. The "again" was kind of a high-pitched whine like a violinist tuning a string. Then suddenly he stopped. A weird look clouded his face and he looked morosely out over the lake.

"How the hell did you know where to look for me?" he wheezed.

"Observation and patience" I quipped. "You went and left tracks on the water. The bubbles from your boat led me from the launch site to the lake. Then they kinda disappeared until they showed up again near these cat tails." I felt that the old fellow deserved at least something of an explanation!

This elicited another bout of ranting and raving, focusing mostly on how dumb he was rather than offering a colorful description of my ancestry. Finally it petered out, giving me the opportunity to instruct him to move the tarp aside. More cursing and swearing, a sure indication that he had done something that he knew to be wrong. Sure enough, there was a pile of fish nets, but no sign of any fish. That prompted a convoluted story about his just going out for a morning spin in his boat and how he had forgotten he had the nets on board. I held up my hand like a traffic policeman, signaling to him that he should stop. Amazingly he did. The reminder that he could be liable for an additional charge of withholding evidence from a fisheries' officer when his case came up in court seemed to stifle him. Especially before a judge already acquainted with his nefarious activities, I emphasized. My directions for him to move the nets brought five boxes of fish into view, all nice-sized walleye. Like an old scratched-up audio tape, he began again, a whining lament something about "not another ticket, I just finished paying for the last one."

The routine, familiar to both of us, continued. As at our last encounter, I outlined to him he faced the loss of his boat, his motor, his nets and his fish, all over and above the fine for this particular offence if he was to be found guilty. This launched him off into another tirade about the injustices of life and so forth. When I began laughing at him, he decided it was time to quit. There is, of course, some danger in laughing; some people just do not see the humor in receiving a ticket, but Bill was harmless in that sense, he was just a slow learner!

25 ~ WINTER GHOST.

No question about it, thieves and poachers know no bounds when it comes to imagination. That imagination comes into play when they are caught with hard evidence in hand and they endeavor to portray themselves as the model citizens they are not!

Everybody knows the magnificent Snowy Owl is a revered winter resident in northern Alberta. Majestic and stately, they are a presence unto themselves. Their relationship with people can best be described as arms-length, yet as they become scarcer, some people develop a fatal attraction for them. Legally or illegally acquired, they have become a trophy so prized that poachers will go to incredible lengths to get one. This in turn has led to their demise in large numbers. The spectacular white and black spotted female is the largest and most sought after of all.

Up in the High Level- Zama Lake area of the province, there was an abundance of Snowy Owls. Unhappily, this fact clashed with a period of massive petroleum development which brought in an array of unsavory characters for whom the word "extinction" meant little if it came to the chance of acquiring a specimen. I had received numerous reports of Snowy Owls being shot but I was always unable to put together quite enough evidence to make a viable prosecution, and that made me very frustrated.

One morning , I was walking down to the local garage to pick up my truck which had been in for minor repair. As I rounded the corner of the garage, I noticed four or five fellows standing around the open trunk of a late model car. One of them was using hand gestures that appeared to describe flight of some sort. As I got closer, the phrase "you should have seen it fly" caught my attention. That was the moment when one of the members of the group noticed me because he was facing in my direction. A frantic gesture to his companions saw all chatter cease and the trunk lid suddenly slam shut. Immediately, the group began to disperse.

Naturally, I was now very curious as to what was in the trunk, you know how that "instinct thing" kicks in. The guy who had been demonstrating flight was making rapidly for the driver's door when I got there. I got between him and the door handle and asked to see what he had in the trunk. He objected angrily.

"Who the hell do you think you are?" he shouted. "You do not have any right to search my vehicle. You aren't a bloody cop, you know!"

This outburst precipitated a little discussion about how his company's name was emblazoned on the vehicle's door and how impressed they were going to be when they heard their company vehicle was under seizure and had been impounded by the Fish and Wildlife division to be searched.

It never ceased to amaze me how quickly the most stubborn of people suddenly see the light when forced to admit they are in the wrong and do not want nor need their bosses to find out what they have been up to, probably on company time to boot.

"Okay, okay, so I'm a wildlife collector." With that, the man opened the trunk. There was a female Snowy Owl, a more perfect specimen one could hardly imagine. Further discussion revealed, before leaving for home down south, he planned to get himself a Snowy Owl if he got the chance. In his trunk was a 12 gauge shotgun, with a box of light shot so as not to spoil the bird for mounting. Nobody carries a shotgun and light bird shot in their vehicle in mid-January.

Seizures were made, tickets written, a bit more success in the war against poachers.

26. OF BEARS AND NAPS

In the late Sixties, what became an annual tradition started on the Peace River, from the town of Peace River down to Tompkins Landing. Game wardens from High Level would meet biologists and game wardens from Peace River and Manning at the mouth of the Notikewin River. One boat would leave Peace River with the Peace River and Manning staff aboard. Another would leave from Tompkins Landing with the High Level staff plus any other interested parties. Usually undertaken in the first or second week of May, the purpose of these patrols was to check on beaver trapping activity and the carryings-on, legal and otherwise, of bear hunters in the general vicinity. At this particular time of year, beavers are highly vulnerable because of their instinctive need to travel. Such behavior is never lost on poachers nor on licensed trappers, but especially not on game wardens, for obvious reasons. It has to be said however, most licensed trappers were conscientious about staying within their designated boundaries. It was the ones who strayed, and of course the poachers, who claimed most of our attention.

The bear hunters, on the other hand, were quite another story. At that time, in the late Sixties, there were not a lot of bear hunters on that stretch of river. And generally, the ones we did get to check were well-behaved. At the same time, there were an awful lot of bears, mostly two year olds, many mothers and cubs. The one and two year olds could often be spotted from afar; their favorite haunt was a perch at the top of a black poplar where they liked to gorge themselves on the buds. Such bears were small, but they were legal. If you saw one at the top of a tree and you made the decision to get a little closer, beaching your boat and hiking up to the site would almost certainly get you a look at some other bears. They all seemed to hang around together, even the older and bigger ones that could never make it up to the buds without breaking the branches and falling to the ground.

On one of these spring patrols, I had a member of the local constabulary for company. I knew I would be in for some unexpected sport when he told me he had never been in a boat on the river.

"Well now, fancy that," I said, a mischievous gleam in my eye.

We launched our 14 foot boat powered by its 35 h.p. outboard motor at Tompkins Landing. The very first swirl we hit made the boat list like it might like to flip over. Now this feeling of listing is always magnified out of all proportion if you have never been in a boat on the river- you are not paying the amount of attention you should, and you are bent over looking for something insignificant on the floorboards and you hit a major swirl. Yes of course, I spotted his awkward posture and could not resist taking advantage by steering in the direction of the list. Well......his reaction was immediate, he tried to sit up! A combination of gravity and inertia halted that. His sudden desperation caused his adrenalin to kick in and the next thing I knew he was all over me. Now we really were listing! And taking water in over the gunwales. Thank goodness the gear was all tied down and stayed put. With a colossal effort, I twisted the steering in an attempt to right the boat. We were literally propelled out of that swirl like a rocket and I was able to regain some control; apparently my adrenalin was working overtime too. A heady mix of luck, adrenalin, and an exotic selection of words my friend had never heard before persuaded him it would be wise to reclaim his seat. I was pleased, even smug; he just looked scared and kept glowering at me as if his unfortunate decision to get into a boat with a known madman was all my fault!

"There you go," I said self-righteously. "You've got to pay close attention when you're on the river." I'm laughing my head off inside, trying to keep a straight face. This fellow was going to be fun all right!

As we proceeded upstream towards the mouth of the Notikewin, we saw bears at every turn, and then some in between. We had a seventy mile trip ahead of us at a maximum speed of 25 m.p.h. So it got to after lunch when my companion decided he needed to go scouting for bears. We snuck in behind some islands where the width of the channel was about the length of the boat, somewhere around fourteen feet. Branches from massive trees arched overhead and reached down into the water, an excellent spot to scare the bejabers out of a first-timer. The trick was to ensure the motor was set on "release" so when you hit a submerged object, usually a deadhead, the motor will kick itself out of the water avoiding critical damage, at least that was what all the commercials said. The sudden noise of the engine roaring in the air is enough to encourage any unfamiliar boatman to take evasive action. This time though,

I decided to "keep my powder dry" as they say, for as yet the policeman was too much of an unknown quantity.

He leaped out on- to the bank and we immediately found a trail snaking its way up the 300 hundred foot incline and into a Fall moose camp. The walking was easy but steep. However, halfway up, my companion had seemingly exercised enough that his anal sphincter needed some urgent relief. Fair enough, I left him to do his business while I continued my way to the top looking for bear sign. I waited, and waited, and waited. Half an hour went by and I was still alone. What could have happened? I mean, all he had to do was to relieve himself, right? I decided I had better make my way down and take a look. Maybe a bear got him at an inopportune moment; bears were always so unpredictable, and this was prime bear country.

I started back down the river bank, keeping myself very much in view on the trail so I could not be mistaken for anything other than a human. I almost made it back to the spot where I had left him, and there was still not the slightest trace of him! This was becoming a little alarming, what on earth could have happened to him? As I headed further down, I finally spied a small hump on the trail further down. Something was curled up in a ball right in the center of the trail. What the hell was it? I hauled out my binoculars and the bundle came into sharp focus. It was him! That son of a gun had gone to sleep right in the middle of the trail, his rifle lying beside him. Going to sleep at the start of his own announced bear hunt, this was intolerable and should be dealt with severely!

"Now what shall I do?" I muttered almost gleefully. I could not let this one pass me by, no sir, but still I had to anticipate any wild reaction from him. "Uh huh, that'll work for me," I thought, "and I shouldn't get myself shot doing it."

Off came my pack, allowing me complete freedom to skulk around in the bush. I paralleled the trail as quietly as a cougar, gliding my way stealthily towards the still sleeping hunter. Murphy's Law, sticks, stones, any useful projectiles are never at hand when you need them. Ah, at last, I came across a fallen aspen with dead branches of just about the right size. I was now in a position where I could see the sleeper but not so close that he would be able to hear me. The wind rustling the aspen leaves, was blowing away from him and towards me so I could simultaneously break off my branches and continue my approach. I got to within about thirty feet, perfectly placed behind a large tree, concealing me entirely. I peered around the tree; he was out for the count.

The first stick landed a mite short. The throw was too tentative, but then one had to be unusually careful when throwing sticks at a hunter asleep on the trail in bear country, especially when his rifle is clearly at hand. Hence my bullet-proof tree.

Second stick. Right over the top of him.

Third stick. This one hit him on the leg. Nothing more than a minor twitch, and that was all. I had been trying not to hit him in the head, but maybe that would be the only thing that would work.

Aha! The next one connected, hit him where the neck and shoulders meet. What impressive reactions, what incredible speed! He rolled over like they always do in a good western and in an instant, he was in the prone position, his rifle in his hands ready to shoot. Only, one thing was wrong- he was facing the wrong way. He was facing away from me.

So help me, I could not stop myself, I absolutely had to throw another stick. Away it went. I aimed it for the bush further up the trail and behind him, out of his field of vision so that he would hear the noise but see no stick. Man, did it ever work! In a flash, he had spun around on his belly. This time, he was right on, his rifle at the ready. Now I had his undivided attention, it came to me that this might be a good time to end the charade. But one more thing, how to make a noise like a bear? On second thoughts.......maybe not such a good idea. A voice from the wilderness took over instead.

"That was a mighty long crap," my voice boomed out. Immediately, he adjusted his posture to face the tree.

"What the hell are you doing going to sleep in the middle of your own bear hunt?" my voice boomed again.

The response was muffled, something about some "inconsiderate expletive deletive not respecting nature". One thing was certain, he was not terribly thrilled so I steered the ensuing conversation to a discussion about the usefulness of continuing on to the top. I explained I saw no bear sign so we returned to the boat once I retrieved my pack. So there we were, not quite halfway to our destination, cruising down the Peace River where little had changed since the days when dugout canoes and rickety rafts were the only mode of travel.

"There are bears over there in those trees," announced my passenger. "See them, halfway up that bank?"

I'd seen them all right. It was just that part of me was hoping he would not see them because we were beginning to run short of time. For me at any rate, it would be nice to get settled into camp before dark. But he was not to be denied, not with a vista of five different bears all atop trees in a hundred square yard patch of bush. So I said we "could take a quick look". Well, you know what always happens when you start that "quick look" stuff? It never works out, does it?

We beached our craft and set off, this time both of us carrying a rifle. We got up close to the bears in the trees and of course Mister Nimrod is desperate to shoot one of them. It was all I could do to convince him they really were too small and there had to be some bigger ones around. Off we went, creeping through the bush and around a clump of trees. And then we saw him. Down in a treed draw with a bald hump sat a medium size bear. Range, about a hundred yards max. Unfortunately, there were no trees handy that the shooter could use as a rest. He insisted adamantly he had to have one, and I was not about to deny him in his excitement, simply because I had no desire to go chasing after a wounded bear if he should foul up. Lying prone would not work because of the sloping ground. There was only one thing to do. I sat down in front of him, allowing him to place the barrel of his gun over my shoulder and out past my face. Yes, you had better believe it; after the trick I had played on him a couple of hours before, I was wondering just how smart this was! I put my fingers in my ears and waited. And waited. And waited some more. I was just beginning to wonder whether he had metamorphosed into a moth when BANG! The bear dropped as it was supposed to. Well wasn't that peachy? It rolled into the brush at the bottom of the hillock. We waited a further five minutes before deciding to take a cautious closer look. The bear was dead, which for me was the ultimate end. But then came the flip-side; on this day, it amounted to a long, slow curse. Picture yourself skinning a large animal in eighty degree heat, with every kind of biting fly insect ever recorded intent on flying up your nostrils or into your mouth. If you have never experienced such a scenario, forgive me but you haven't lived. Besides, the sun was now choosing to set, which encouraged us to complete the skinning in record time. We carried the hide down to the boat, salted it with two 1 lb. Boxes of table salt, and rolled it up into a plastic bag. From there it was placed up in the bow of the boat on the floorboards, the intrepid hunter hardly able to tear his excited eyes away from his trophy.

We had to look forward to another hour of threading our way upriver before we hit the campsite. But it proved to be a fabulous trip. The sun setting behind us bathed us and all around with an extraordinary light. We found we could see into every nook and cranny with the utmost clarity. Even the bears in the trees appeared as if they were highlighted in some supernatural way. Certainly it was hard to keep track of their numbers, they were simply everywhere!

Eventually we made it to the mouth of the Notikewin River. Wouldn't you know it, the others were already there, tents up, fire going, supper cooking. They had traveled in a handcrafted wooden river boat boasting a 50 h.p. Mercury and a spare 20 h.p. Mercury outboard for power. Yet when loaded up with all the gear, the personnel, and the extra gas, it was woefully underpowered. "Captain Sandbar" was both captain and navigator; you can surely guess how he got that name!

Boy, those city boys sure knew all about eating a hearty meal outdoors on the river! They had room for coolers storing bacon, eggs, steak, and all the gastronomic trimmings. And of course, there was the special cooler designed for spirits, assuredly not the kind you would expect to see in a church.

We busied ourselves unloading our own gear and setting up our tent before sitting down to a tasty supper. There were all of the day's activities to talk about, with a few extra lies thrown in for color commentary, I was certain of that. Apparently the behavior of those trappers who were approached by them had been exemplary, although it had to be acknowledged in this particular year, there were far fewer hunters than usual. The only circumstance coming across as somewhat out of the ordinary was the sighting of a very small boat operated by an unidentified person hightailing it the other way the moment he, or she, was spotted. As always, one of the main topics of conversation was the weather. For the other crew, the heat had been intense at some of the stops they had made to check out trappers' cabins. One cabin had an exotic collection of thermometers all registering somewhere between 100 and 105 F., a little hotter than where we had hailed from.

The next morning, we started back downstream towards Tompkins Landing. But before we could leave, our infamous fishery biologist had his work to do. We got talking about a small craft training course I had been on and I found myself explaining that objects under water in rivers do not necessarily follow the same direction as the current on the surface. In the context of the course, it was" bodies" they were talking about. We wanted to explore this notion further and since nobody offered themselves up as a potential victim of drowning, we caught ourselves a sucker. Yes, I know suckers can swim in whatever direction they desire, but it seemed more fun than tagging along behind a water-logged length of tree trunk. The fish-tagging expertise of our biologist was put to good use; he attached a two foot length of fishing line to the appropriate spot close to the base of the fish's dorsal fin. To this he tied an inflated condom. Now we could track the movements of the fish without even raising a sweat. Carefully, we put the sucker back into the river. Immediately, it swam off into deep water, so we hastily prepared our boats to follow. Just as we were casting off, we spotted the condom on its way back. In all, we consumed about 45 minutes in observation; clearly it was we who were the suckers! And the fish that should have been so honored to be part of such a revolutionary scientific experiment? All it did was swim around in a 30 square yard area. Somewhat chastened, we caught our friend, removed the line and the condom, set it free and got on our way.

"Why would a game warden be carrying a condom on river patrol?" you ask.

"They're like boy scouts," I am driven to reply. "Always ready and prepared to assist in any enterprise that comes their way, as in a biological experiment for example. Let's leave it at that."

Part of our assignment on this year's trip was to assist the Fish and Wildlife biologist in overnight netting at the mouths of creeks to determine fish species, weights, sexes, population densities, that sort of thing. This was to be the next item on the agenda.

164

The gear all packed up and stowed away, we found ourselves on the way to the Little Buffalo and Keg rivers. En route, we saw numerous bears in trees and on the shoreline; one was even swimming the river but made a quick exit as we approached. When they are wet, it is very difficult to determine how big they are. The consensus on our swimmer was it was a three year old. Then we were back doing that "behind-the-island" thing again, constantly checking for signs of recent activity. We drifted past isolated trapper's cabins, once somebody's idea of paradise, perhaps a place where they had chosen to live to avoid the rat race and live out a different lifestyle, one amounting to an abandonment of the day for the simplicity of the 1920s or the 1950s. Unhappily, our busy schedule would not allow for further investigation. Another time.

Everything was unfolding as it should, and with our detours into the back channels we came across the odd skittish deer, many ducks and geese, and even the occasional clumsy moose. It was as if we had been lulled into a false sense of security, for which we were soon to pay a price. We were almost to the end of the final island in a long string, and were narrowly separated from the shore by the merest sliver of a channel. Our conversation was rudely interrupted by a thunderous roar, just the kind you hear when your propeller and lower unit have connected with a submerged something or other. Instantly, we both glanced back to see a huge plume of water at the stern. There was the motor, horizontal to the boat, not vertical as it was supposed to be. As quickly as it happened, the roar abated and the motor was back in the water, still running smoothly. Aha, bitter experience told me certain things might have been bent.

We beached the craft stern first. Fortunately, there was no damage to the reinforced stern nor to the lower leg of the motor, but the propeller was an outright mess. Aluminum props bend very easily but are "field flexible" with nature's tool shop. So I removed the prop and, using a rounded boulder as an anvil and another as a hammer, I pounded it back into some semblance of its original shape. I was almost done when, wouldn't you know it, Captain Sandbar showed up. Well, he was nothing but a bag of laughs and guffaws, as were his cohorts. So much for team effort, I thought sullenly. There were wise cracks about excessive speed, excessive proximity to immovable objects like the river bottom, and the chronic inability of some navigators to see far enough ahead to know where they were going. The real truth however, lay in the fact the river went down about a foot since our journey upstream, and that had been just enough to cause trouble. The prop, now more of an artist's rendering of its real self, was reinstalled and off we went again. Naturally, our top speed had diminished somewhat because of the missing chunks of aluminum on the prop. I have to say it did look as though a hungry beaver had been chewing on it.

We passed the only still occupied hamlet on the map between Peace River and Fort Vermilion, a place called Carcajou. Surveyed somewhere around 1914, four blocks with 20 lots to the block, somebody must have had a mighty rosy view of its future prosperity. One of the only inhabitants left on this day was the store owner who handled the mail and some of everything you never saw before, plus the odd everyday item. The only buildings left standing were the owner's attached residence and some outbuildings, an old schoolhouse which had subsequently become home to a

John Deere combine, and a Catholic Church. It seems after the Mackenzie Highway #35 was constructed, most of the Carcajou inhabitants chose to move across the river to be near the highway and therefore town.

When we made it to the Little Buffalo River, a high and dry location up in the willows became our campsite. Some of the willows were cleared, a fire pit was constructed, and most important of all, water for the tea was put on the boil while the grill was being set up to cook supper. Our decision to eat first made the setting of nets a bit late but still we hoped to get an adequate sample of fish nonetheless. Soon the fire was just right for sitting around and telling tall tales, perfect for banishing the mosquitoes and heating the tea, and with enough light to guide the net setters to our landing. Inevitably the consumption of hot tea and even warmer spirits continued on late into the night.

The next morning clarified it was the spirit drinkers who were a little slow getting up. A frenzied bout of wood cutting with the chain saw quickly changed their attitude. But hold on a second, there was one holdout, one inert body that seemed comatose........and who do you think it was?

That's right! It was the same guy who went to sleep on the trail when we were hunting bears. Clearly, there was only one solution for such decadence. Four of us grabbed him, still in his sleeping bag, and dragged him out of his tent. Once outside, we shook the bag to ensure that he remained well down inside it, and then we headed for the river. Somehow procrastinators always seem to know when they are in imminent danger. This one sure did, but all of his struggles were in vain. Furthermore, he quickly sensed we were headed for the river with a good deal of malicious intent. It was at the bank the real negotiations began. We commenced the obligatory swinging and the count to three to ensure we were coordinated enough to heave him a respectable distance into the water. The obscenities emanating from the bag were now turning the air bluer than the smoke from the fire.

"We're counting for real now," someone announced grandly. "One." The bag swung out over the water.

"I'll do the dishes, and make the fires," the muffled voice pleaded his case from the inside of the bag.

"Two," announced our spokesman as the second swing took our victim back out over the flow.

"Guys, I really will. I promise." The voice was now in panic mode.

You will surely think we were too soft on him, but that assertion saved his butt. Business was resumed, breakfast eaten, and the net setters set off to pull their nets. The rest of us set to, cleaning up the camp and gathering wood.

Two hours later, the net pullers showed up with 300 pounds of fish. So much for setting the nets late, we had been hoping for maybe half that amount. The sheer volume called for a production line of sorts. "The scientist", that was his nickname, was in charge. Every fish had to be weighed, measured and sexed, after which scales samples were taken. A volunteer whose writing did not resemble a drunken spider doodling in the ink, recorded all of this information. Those of us not involved in the production line gassed up the motors and cleaned the boats in readiness for the next leg of our journey, all the while monitoring any traffic on the river, at an all-time low this particular year. Game wardens are always keenly interested in who their neighbors are, human or animal, so of course we had to check out the river bank for sign of whatever type . Animal tracks were abundant, everything from bear to moose to deer to mink. Birds too were well represented with geese, shore birds and all kinds of duck. As for humanity, nobody except us.

We made our way back to the production line. Hmm, it was humming along just a little too smoothly. "The scientist" had the "weight thing" down pat. That he was guessing the weight of every fish to within two or three ounces was simply unacceptable; something had to be done about it! A quick unobtrusive strategy session was convened. For starters, we needed a long slim rock. Then we had to sneak a specimen away from the pile of fish that was well within "the scientist's" peripheral vision. Distracted by some very obviously meaningful gestures to his recorder, we achieved our objective unseen and got ourselves a fish. We popped open the fish's mouth and inserted the rock. More by good luck than good design, it fit right down inside so that it would not fall out if the fish was held upside down..........or so we hoped. Another series of meaningful gestures again distracted our biologist friend so we could return our fish back to the pile. Then we waited, and waited. We watched in disbelief as he took every fish around it, treating it as if it was highly contaminated. Had he tumbled to our little scheme, we wondered. No! Finally he grabbed it by the tail. Oh crap! No, it was okay, the rock had stayed in. Across to the measuring board he went.

"Holy cow!" he announced. "This little sucker is sure heavy for his size. Must have been eating rocks or something." Now how creative, how coincidental was that?

Asked to guess the weight, and much to everyone's surprise, he came extremely close for a rock-filled fish, missing the exact weight by only five ounces. Then came the sexing. When you do this, you have to split the skin and the belly meat to expose the internal organs, Normally, this can be done without cutting the stomach, yet it becomes less and less likely if you have just done some 200 fish and your hands are getting tired. Sure enough, like the little boys we often were, we were easily and instantly amused when we heard what we had been waiting for all this time, the rasping of a finely honed blade on rock.

"What the.....?" was all we got out of "the scientist". What a supreme disappointment he had turned out to be. He calmly reached for the sharpening stone and did what any self-righteous adult would do in the company of delinquent juveniles; he re-honed his knife and carried on, though not before giving us a look of withering contempt. Well, you can only do what you can I guess; it wasn't as if we didn't try!

When the biologist had finished collecting the required data, the fish were loaded on to a boat and taken upstream to be dumped on the bank to be consumed by the local scavengers, that is all but the ones we were inclined to use for taste testing. They were very good, needless to say. The remainder of the day was uneventful, a real drag if truth be known, with the return to Tompkins Landing the next day to look forward to.

The final morning was a surprise. First of all, everybody was up. The "self-appointed" fire maker and dishwasher did his job unasked and unaided. We ate and broke camp in true team-like fashion.

When we arrived at Tompkins Landing, the Manning and Peace River staff were happy to see their truck and trailer waiting as if on cue. All the driver had to do was decide exactly where the best place to land would be, back his trailer into the water, winch the boat on to the trailer, and they could all go home to domestic bliss. But who decreed this journey was to be straight forward? The truck driver was inexperienced in the art of landing river boats and chose a site that was much too soft. Not that there was necessarily a better site, I must confess. The river had gone down way below normal, the river boat was not the size of your average dinghy, and the landing spot was a gooey mess. Our saving grace and rescue appeared in the form of the Caterpillar used to maintain the ferry landing. Because the truck had to back the trailer in far enough to load the boat, it was mired beyond hope. Not a problem for the Cat. Out she came, boat and all. Of course, being the true gentleman that he was, the Cat operator did the same for me.

Oh, the bear hide? It was a beauty. Home-tanned, it was made into a magnificent rug.

27 ~ MULTICOLORED SNOW!

Once in a while, you get the last laugh when you least expect it, and sometimes that laugh is as good as, or better, than any monetary bonus. There I was, driving around north of High Level on a cool crisp February day doing the game warden thing, you know, on the lookout for signs of illegal hunting, trapping and so forth. This day, my focus was on the ptarmigan hunters. The season was already open and my mission was to make sure nobody was giving in to temptation to shoot from the highway. Usually it was only the most indolent of hunters who would do this, but the practice was not only illegal, it was also highly dangerous. The ptarmigan were naturally attracted to the highway where they could peck at the gravel, a great temptation for those hunters who found the act of walking too much of a chore. At the same time, I was also interested in which trappers might be accessing their trap lines from the highway, and the general state of the moose population in the area.

With no need to hurry, I was dawdling along at patrol speed, 40 m.p.h., and generally minding my own business when a half ton truck appeared in my rearview mirror. I had just come round a corner and was looking down a two to three mile straight stretch of highway. There at the far end was a grader, traveling in the same direction as I was and removing snow from the edge of the road. All of a sudden, the truck, that a few seconds ago had not been much more than a blob in my mirror, was right beside me. Not only that, he was making gestures at me indicating he wanted to race. Immediately, I recognized him as the manager of one of the local restaurants. He brazenly continued alongside, his gestures still going through the "let's race" motions. I held my up my hand flat on my side window in the conventional stop signal and mouthed the word "no". Not content with that, he waved his hand in the "ah, come on you chicken" signal. I responded with an even more emphatic no and he took off, spinning his wheels in disgust as he left. I kept on driving and looking for animal sign, dismissing the fellow as one of those kooks born every day.

Nothing unusual in the bush so I looked up to check the road ahead. The racing freak was closing up fast to both the grader and the far corner. Just then my eye picked up a movement in the bush; it was just another moose browsing peacefully among the willows. Another check was due to reaffirm where I was going. That was the instant I realized I was in for some drama. Speedy Gonzales was right behind the grader when another half ton appeared round the corner and heading in the opposite direction. At a distance of two or so miles, it was difficult, if not impossible to judge exactly how close the two trucks and the grader actually were to each other. However, even I could see they were uncomfortably close.

As if on cue, my concerns were borne out very dramatically. Speedy's brake lights suddenly came on. I saw him pull out to pass the grader and then pull back in again.

Almost instantaneously, he was doing doughnuts in the middle of the road and then back in behind the grader. The oncoming vehicle had wisely slowed down to a crawl on its side of the road, moving along slowly almost in the ditch.

The whole performance ended in a huge cloud of white snow billowing out of the ditch just behind the grader; the racing man slid half sideways, half backwards into the ditch on his side of the road. With my usual warped sense of humor, I found the spectacle to be nothing short of hilarious. I mean, how often do you come across a "Testosterone Tim" wanting to race you? Then, after you have turned him down, how often would you have the pleasure of seeing him explode off into the ditch? This day, I was more than doubly blessed for the best was yet to come.

When I arrived on the scene, the grader operator and the two drivers were standing behind the grader. The operator's conversation was very animated. As I opened my door, I heard a series of "expletive deletives" about some damn nutcase blasting into the rear wheel of his grader and pitching the operator forward on to his controls, then spinning around in the middle of the road like a unbalanced top. Did the "expletive deletive" not know he could have caused a major accident, the operator fumed. Ah hah, so that was why old Speedy was doing such spectacular doughnuts behind the grader, he had actually hit it! No wonder the operator was so angry, you have to hit a grader pretty hard to throw the operator forward like that. What could Speedy say in his defense? Nothing. But he did contrive to look sheepish and apologetic at the same time. And he had the eminent good sense not to say anything. That was when we all turned round to look at his truck. It was stuck backwards in the ditch, the back half of the box almost totally submerged in snow. But this was no ordinary snow, this was "pressurized, carbonated" snow. In some places, it was slowly turning orange, in other places a sort of caramel brown. When you are hauling supplies to a restaurant, and when those supplies include pressurized containers of pop, it is not a good idea to make a detour into the ditch at any time or you may end up dying the snow.

A great believer in that old adage" one should never deny ones own personality", I could not resist a comment to the racer, more of a question really, something about whether he still wanted a race. An unmistakable message from a man of over six feet and more than two hundred pounds, together with a visual gesture as to how this might be accomplished, told me I had won the day. Best of all, there was no harm done, except perhaps to one overblown ego.

28. DEAD MOOSE WALKING

It was in the middle of supper, it was always in the middle of supper, when the phone rang. Minus 40 degrees F, High Level, and here I was looking forward to a cozy evening at home.

"Are you the game warden?" queried the gruff voice on the line.

"Yes. As a matter of fact I am."

"Well some s.o.b. has gone and stolen our moose."

Now this was a new one for me; I did not know quite what to say.

"Are you there?" the voice asked impatiently.

"Yes. Yes, I'm here. How the hell does somebody go about stealing somebody else's moose?"

"Simple. I'm down at the hotel. Some s.o.b. drives up and steals my moose from in front of the quonset that is behind the hotel, you know the one."

"Yeah, I know the one. Maybe you had better wait right where you are. I'll be right down." Another fine meal interrupted. "Goes with the territory I suppose," I thought to myself. At least my truck was still relatively warm from my afternoon patrol.

Five minutes to the only hotel in town, a veritable hive of extra-curricular activity. The bar was about to close for an hour so great care had to be exercised to avoid running over any of the evicted and/or disgruntled patrons. To put this into historical perspective, the incident occurred in those heady days of Social Credit government in Alberta in the sixties. The law stipulated that all drinkers and other like-minded sinners should go home and eat supper with their families; the bar was officially closed for one hour, as if that would do any good! Looking over this motley collection of individuals, I found myself wondering how many of them actually made it home.

I had not taken two steps into the restaurant before three guys approached me, accosted me would be a better way to put it. I hoped one of them was the caller because I had no real desire to hang around this place any longer than I had to. They certainly appeared to be upset.

"You the game warden?" That same gruff voice, now emanating directly from a personality that seemed equally as abrasive as the voice.

"Yes I am. Are you the fellow that just phoned my house?"

"I did," barked the man as if even words should be economized.

I took over, and we all introduced ourselves formally and then headed out to the quonset. It turned out these were three hunters from central Alberta who had hunted in the area before. Apparently one of them was part owner of the hotel which they used as a base for their hunting activity.

"So what's the story?"

That was the cue for the second, more pushy fellow to launch into a detailed description starting from the moment they had crawled out of bed that morning. Enamored of his own voice, and evidently quite the man with words, he was determined to leave no stone unturned. Clearly, the others were used to this; they just let him ramble on. Leaving town by snowmobile, they had decided to head west to an area where they were successful in previous years. They had not gone very far before they chanced on some fresh moose sign. They got "real excited", the man said, and abandoned their machines so that they could track their quarry on foot. The words flowed fast and furious with a special emphasis for the dramatic; hell, the way he went on, anybody would have thought they baited a king-size grizzly. For three hours, they had not just walked but battled through two feet of snow. They had toiled over and under scattered piles of deadfall and other debris. They had fought their way through thickets of uncooperative willow when suddenly one of them had been presented with the perfect opportunity to shoot. The moose had gone down and the real work began.

The shooter stayed to field dress the moose while his two buddies went back for the snowmobiles. Since they had to resort to chainsaws to make some sort of a trail through the willows and the deadfall in order to get a snowmobile in and the moose out, they were gone quite some time. Fortunately for them, they happened on a seismic line cut through the bush so their trail building was suddenly reduced to a minimum. What complicated their plan was they wanted to bring the moose back whole, that is only its intestines removed. That way, they figured they could skin and quarter it in the comfort of the quonset. I did not suppose it had anything to do with the minus 40 F weather, or did it? With lots of track spinning, complemented with plain old pushing, pulling, and shoving, they got their moose back to town in one piece. But they had all worked up a monstrous appetite, and what do you know, there was this restaurant right next to the quonset. The temptation was simply too great; they unhooked their snowmobiles and left the moose in the driveway of the quonset.

You already know what happened then, or you guessed it. The whole moose was stolen while they were eating supper not fifty yards away. To say they were incensed was an understatement, they were white hot with anger. Had they caught the thief, they would have lynched him on the spot without a second thought. If only to calm them down, I decided to go through all the motions, knowing all the time my chances of finding a moose that was now probably well on its way to being consigned to someone's freezer, were slim to none. I took down a description of where the animal had been shot, the size of the antlers and body, that sort of thing.

"Do you think you can find it for us?" quizzed the wordy one hopefully.

"Well, this is definitely a different one," I stalled. "You can see the dual wheel truck marks that back up to where you guys left the moose. See how the moose was skidded here and then lifted up on to the truck? Has to be a one or two ton truck with gin poles. There are plenty of them around here."

A little explanation; gin poles are two hollow steel pipes, approximately eight feet long that are pinned to the back of the truck deck, one on each side. When they are not in use, they rest in beds on the outer edge of the deck. The pins allow the poles to be brought together over the deck of the truck where a pulley can be pinned between them. Quite simply, a stationary cable is attached to the peak of the gin poles and down to the truck to anchor them at a predetermined angle above the deck. You run your deck winch cable up over the pulley and down to your load, start your winch and voila, you are in business.

Clearly the hunters were naive enough to have hope. "How, how long would it take for this guy to back in here and load it like you said? I mean hell, we only left the moose for around half an hour". The spokesman expressed enough frustration for all three of them.

"If the gin poles are already set up and ready to go, all you have got to do is run your cable to the moose, hook on to it, and haul it up on to the truck. So probably less than five minutes." I really did not want to get their hopes up; the last thing I wanted them to think was it would be easy to solve this case.

"We would have to have been right here to catch them then?"

"Yeah, that's right. I'll make some enquiries tonight. How long are you boys going to be around?"

"Oh, two or three more days," the gruff one took over. "You know, it was my tag on that moose, and now I am left without either a moose or a tag. Would it be possible for me to get another tag at least?"

"Give me time to think about that," I said carefully, not wanting to make it seem easy. "Come on down to the office tomorrow morning and I will let you know."

"Okay, it's a deal." He turned away.

I went home and made some phone calls as promised. Would you believe that a red two-ton with dual wheels was spotted on the north side of town? Not only that, there was a moose hanging from the gin poles, all at the same time the moose disappeared. Not that anybody could see the license plate, it was too dark. Why would anybody be that interested anyway? After all, a moose on the back of a truck or hanging from a set of gin poles would attract very little attention in these parts. I did what I had to do, I called the local constabulary and asked them to keep an eye open for the truck and the moose. Then I went for a leisurely drive around town. I'd had no idea there were that many red one-ton and two-ton trucks with gin poles around town. And that was at night. How many more would there be in the daytime?

Next morning, down at the office, the hunter turned up as expected. No, he decided he did not want another tag, not that this made him any less angry with what had happened.

"Well, you wanted to know if I had any chance whatsoever of catching whoever stole your moose. I have to tell you now that it looks highly unlikely. Hopefully someone will talk, that's my best chance."

"Fine," he said, resigning himself to reality. "Do what you can. You have my phone number. I'll talk to you again." They left town to resume hunting since the others still had their tags.

Something prompted me to go for another drive to see if I could find a more likely red truck with gin poles. How fortunate, one local company had a whole fleet of trucks that fitted the description. The more I looked, the more I found, and found out about! I checked all of the trucks I found for any sign of a moose having been recently hauled on them. Not a hair in sight. I have to confess there was an "up" side to all of this, in fact two" up sides". One was all of the people to whom I told the story laughed uproariously. The second was the hunters had helped their cause and mine by posting all around town a hundred dollar reward for the recovery of their moose.

My enquiries went on; no luck at all.

Now this whole story happened in late November. The following February, I was waiting for my truck to be repaired at the local garage. A man whom I had never seen before came up to me and started chatting.

"You still looking for that moose, the one that those guys were offering a reward for?"

"Of course," I responded. "Why? Do you know where it is?"

"Yes I do. Let's go talk outside." That was when he told me where it was and whose truck had been used. Who knows why people do what they do? It was hard to believe after so much time had elapsed, someone had decided to come forward and let me know where the moose was. I asked him about the reward and to my utter surprise, he was not in the least bit interested.

So the next move was to verify his story.

According to my informant, it was supposed to be in a house used only in the summer by the farmer on whose land it was located. I discovered the house easily enough. There were no vehicle tracks to it in the snow that separated it from the road fifty yards away. Once again, snowshoe time! I never traveled without them; there is nothing to beat them over snow-drifted terrain. When I got up to the house, I looked through the window to see parts of a moose all over the kitchen table, with other parts on the floor, and all frozen solid because this was a house that remained unheated over winter. But there was one huge problem; since the hunters never made any body shots on their trophy, the discovery of all this meat would probably be for naught.

I went back over the description that the hunters had given me. The only distinguishing details that might be remotely useful were there was a hole in the right antler, and the moose had taken a bullet through the right eye. Therefore it was crucial I find the head. I scanned every room in the house. There was definitely no moose head anywhere inside. Okay, then how about outside? There were no outbuildings to speak of, so where else could I search? There were several groves of trees some distance off. I could certainly take a walk over there but finding a moose head in three feet of snow in a patch of scrub would call for the kind of luck you can only dream about. I had to admit to myself I was clutching at straws.

What was that? On the edge of one clump of trees a couple of hundred yards away, there was what appeared to be an old horse-drawn wagon with a grain box on it. Well, what the hell, since it had piqued my curiosity, I decided to take a closer look at it. When I got up to it, I found myself sinking into the snow that had drifted alongside the grain box, but yet I could still see over the side. Something brown was sticking out of the snow. The snow was much too soft to support anything, so whatever the mysterious thing was, it had to be half buried in there. Oh man, could I be lucky enough that this was the long sought-after moose head? Was that brown thing sticking up a portion of its antlers?

Off came the snowshoes and into the wagon I tumbled. I reached down into the snow and grabbed on to whatever was there and began pulling. Emerging from the snow like the monster from the white lagoon was a large moose head, hole in the right antler, shot through the right eye. Banzai, this was it! Allow me to caution you here about lugging moose heads around the countryside while on snowshoes. It is not recommended and should be avoided at all costs, no matter how robust your heart. But, when you are twenty-something, and it may solve a convoluted case, it had to be done. It was time to head for home.

After some thawing, much cutting and sawing, I removed a bullet embedded in the animal's skull. Naturally I congratulated myself on my previous thoroughness; prior to the departure of the hunters back in November, I had asked them to fire three rounds from the moose hunter's rifle into a keg of water at the local garage so I could retain slug samples on file for the use of forensic staff in the unlikely event I located the moose. I packaged up the three samples together with the one I had removed from the moose's head and sent them off for analysis in accordance with normal procedure. A month later, the results came in; all four slugs had numerous characteristics in common, enough for the forensic staff to testify that the likelihood of them all coming from the same firearm was conclusive as far as they were concerned.

Finding the landowner now became the top priority. This did not take very long as I had been working on that aspect of things already. When I confronted him and broached the subject, he was decidedly unimpressed with everything I had to say. For the life of him, he could not understand the notion that, since the moose head was found on his property, he was in illegal possession, even though he protested loudly he never had anything to do with the animal. Uh huh, so who would go to all the trouble of carrying a great big moose head past his house to a grove of trees two hundred yards beyond and place it in an old disused grain wagon? Oh no, not him, not him! And all that meat in the house? Not him, not him again!

A little more snooping about town soon revealed he had solicited help; I got the name. Wouldn't you know it, he was the owner of the elusive red truck with the gin poles. A chat with him was very illuminating, enough to incriminate the farmer. When I confronted the latter for the second time, he was very loud and very angry, but he said enough for me to write up a ticket and set a date in court.

The day of reckoning finally arrived. Despite the forensic evidence and more, both defendants plead not guilty, a move necessitating a trial down the road. At the trial itself, there was a good turnout. People were genuinely interested in how it would all play out, and for us in the Fish and Wildlife Division, it publicized the fact we were active in the community at large. The prosecutor presented evidence, the defendants presented theirs, and the scales of justice ground slowly into motion. The outcome? Guilty! Plus a fine of $ 100 each, not much for the work done but a clear message to the public nonetheless. And a great deal of satisfaction for me.

As for the moose antlers, they were not gigantic and, to be honest, I cannot remember if the outraged hunter ever came to pick them up in spite of his great enthusiasm on the phone. It would have been a long way to drive just for a set of rather ordinary moose antlers.

29 ~ FISH SNARING

Let's put it this way- we all try to do our best at our chosen profession. In so doing, we need to understand how "the opposition" conducts its business so we, in turn, are forced into making what we do more effective. This principle is as true in the world of Fish and Wildlife as it is in the world of commerce. In our case, we set out to learn as much as we could about how various offences were committed and the all sorts of ingenious techniques and devices used.

Spring in the High Prairie area made it a haven for illegal fishing. After illegal nets, the most popular technique was using a snare. So simple, so effective in skilled hands yet, it was something my partner and I had never tried.

On this particular occasion, we decided to head out to one of the local snaring hot spots. As it came into sight, we approached slowly in our vehicle. We had a clear and uninterrupted view down a straight stretch of road. No vehicles to be seen, probably nobody there. Caution still prevailed. Often people would be dropped off to do the snaring and then be picked up later; the seasoned poachers knew well any collection of parked cars inevitably alerted the prying eyes of the fish cops, so it was better not to attract attention by conducting their activities on foot. No lookout was visible, there was not a soul there! A good time for us to scout around and see how much activity had occurred since our last visit.

Lots! And what was this? A bunch of snare poles?

Sure enough, two willow poles, eight to ten feet long with brass wire loops at the end, your standard snaring gear and not something from the fishing aisle of the nearest Canadian Tire store. Our talk turned to a discussion about how difficult it was to snare. We both heard stories about different styles and what worked best; here was an opportunity to find out for ourselves. We opened the snares up to what appeared to be an appropriate size for the fish we could see. Sometimes, the fish were literally bank to bank; minutes later there would only be one or two. We quickly found that trying to snare fish when they were heavily congested was a waste of time because the loop would quickly get bent out of shape before you had homed in on your target. We found it to be far better to wait until the fish became more spread out. Even then our success was limited, probably due to a lack of practice on our part. The fish would swim their way into the wire loop, or you would ease it over them, just past their gills. A powerful and quick two-handed heave on the pole tightened up the snare, and a solid jerk to the right or left would leave the fish flapping helplessly on the ground. Of course, all of the ones we landed were put back into the creek where they swam off. However, the interesting thing about the practice was the mark you would leave around the fish when you tightened the snare, very distinct and not removable. We put it all down to an interesting and educational experience, the kind of hands-on learning that today would be described as "professional development".

Off we went to check on other hot spots. Four such spots later with nothing to add. Had to be bingo night in town or something! Maybe it was time to recheck the site where we had experimented with the snares. Our first mistake, we did not approach as cautiously as we had before. In the distance, down that straight stretch of road, we saw a movement that looked horribly like a person slinking off into the bush. This prompted our second mistake, an immediate increase in speed, but to no avail. By the time we stopped, there were three innocent-looking people standing on the bank and reeling in their lines. They were quite happy to show us their angling licenses and the fish they had caught. You guessed it! The fish all had snare marks on them.

No amount of questioning would ever get them to admit to using a snare. Oh no, the fish had all been caught on hook and line and curiously, every one of them had snare marks when they were brought in.

"I wonder where those marks could have come from?" I mused out loud, hoping that someone would be gullible enough to incriminate himself. There were no takers.

A short conference with my partner did not resolve much. The bottom line was the fish could have been caught with snare marks already on them, and we would face a hell of a time trying to prove they were not caught on hook and line. We picked up the snare poles as we should have done in the first instance and went disappointedly on our way. The snickering we heard as we departed let us know that we could chalk up one for the bad guys. And yes, you live and learn.

30 ~ WHO LEARNED WHAT FROM WHOM?

Horses and wolves have coexisted in relative harmony since the beginning of time, although wolves have always tended to be the dominant force in the relationship. Some time after Christmas in 1972, a distraught guide, trapper, outfitter, and general all-round woodsman showed up at the Fish and Wildlife office in High Prairie. Trust me, it would take a lot to bring such characters to town, and a lot more for them to venture into a government office. It had to be something really serious for him to be here.

"So what's the great occasion I asked?" surely an appropriate opening since it had to be a momentous occasion to bring him in.

"You're not going to believe this," he said somberly as he sat down.

It seemed that, on the previous day, he went out to where he was pasturing his horses to see how they were surviving one of the harshest winters ever, pawing out an increasingly meager existence on a native pasture along the banks of a creek. This was the same creek he always had to ford twice, whether he was going to town or heading home. The alarm bells started to sound in his head when he found they were not where they usually hung out, so he set off to look for them. He did not have to go far before he stumbled on a scene that left him aghast, a scene with which he was still having great difficulty coming to terms.

"You know, I haven't been around nearly as long as you, and I certainly don't come close to the amount of time that you have spent in the bush," I commented. "But I know a lot of folks and I have talked to a lot of others who have spent all their lives in the bush and I have never come across anything like this."

"Well, I want something done about it! There's no way we can allow it to happen again. I rely on my horses for my living. When can you come out there and take a look?"

"Today won't work. It'll be dark in less than an hour. How about first thing tomorrow morning? It's not supposed to snow tonight, so we should be okay." The poor fellow needed all the encouragement he could get.

"You're sure you know the place I'm talking about? Just down the creek from the first ford? You won't need me there, you can see it all for yourself. Then do whatever you have to do, but make it right."

"Yeah, I know the spot. And thanks for coming in. I'll be sure and let you know what we decide to do."

For those who have never lived in northern Alberta, "first thing in the morning', a time when you can see well enough to follow a set of tracks, might be as late as eight o'clock. And even then, visibility would depend on the weather.

The next morning, my partner and I set off in the truck, the snowmobile loaded in the back. It took us about an hour to get out there, park the truck and begin walking to the site of all the drama. It was truly very interesting, more so because both of us were seasoned students of wolf behavior and neither of us had ever seen or heard of such antics before. The tracks were exactly as the complainant had described them, those of the wolves and those of the horses. After studying the myriad of sign on the ground, we reached the same conclusion as he had.

There was a large knoll of high ground with native grass growing on it, the kind of grass that would surely tickle a horse's fancy. This made it one of their favorite places to graze. The knoll itself had been partially eroded by the creek so a high cliff had formed above the now solid ice on the creek. The cliff was almost vertical, about 25 feet in height, and paralleled the creek for a fair distance before tapering off on both sides back down to the creek bank, three to four feet above the ice.

The story was in the tracks. Starting some distance back from the cliff, there was evidence from the way the horse tracks milled around something had been herding them together. The wolf tracks on the other hand, betrayed a long loping stride urging the horses forward in the same direction, towards the cliff. Clearly there had been six horses in the group; first one set of tracks veered off to the left, then another set to the right until there was apparently only one horse left, on the brink of the cliff. At this point, the wolf tracks converged into a semi-circle, the horse clearly in the middle and backed up to the edge of the cliff. The snow here was churned up with a maze of tracks. Exactly how the wolves got the horse to jump or fall off the cliff was not discernible, but emanating outwards from the maze, the wolf tracks indicated a hasty scramble down both sides of the knoll to a lower spot on the bank, allowing access to the base of the cliff. The horse lay a short distance upstream from where it had tumbled off the cliff, added momentum from the fall perhaps? As we were wont to do, we had to establish the cause of death, as if that were not obvious! Yet we were amazed we could find no external damage whatsoever, no bites on the neck, no hamstringing, no compounded fractures, no broken neck. Rigor mortis and the freezing weather rendered it impractical to establish other possible causes of death. Moreover, there was absolutely no chance of determining from the tracks in the snow what other goings-on had occurred because the snow all around the horse's cadaver was packed solid with wolf prints.

From a short distance behind, the horse looked as though it was just lying there. More thorough inspection revealed classic wolf behavior; entry from the back. They had enlarged the anal opening to a size equivalent to one of their den openings. From here they had apparently "gone inside and cleaned up", so to speak. You may find this part a bit gory, but if one does not look then one cannot say for sure. So I shone my flashlight up inside the horse. There was nothing left but ribs with skin on the outside. It was slick and clean right up to the base of the neck. Seemingly, it is not only us humans who like a hot lunch!

Now a conundrum. The horse owner had asked, demanded that something be done. The carcass was deep in the snow and frozen to the ice preventing the complete scavenging of the rest. Given the circumstances, there was only one logical way for us to deal with the problem; unfortunately, it is nobody's favorite but it was the most cost effective for what we were dealing with. Poison. Coincidentally, that was what the policy manual prescribed for such situations. Rule of thumb suggested that wolves would make a full circuit of their home range once every two weeks. So we baited the horse and took off. Now it was simply a question of monitoring the site from our snowmobiles every few days, making a point to park as far away from the horse as possible. Just as long as we had it in sight, that was all that we needed. Of course, we made very sure that we did not take even one step from our machines when checking after poisoning the carcass . One human footprint in the snow could easily prompt the wolves to change their routine and not return for months on end. This checking procedure went on for the rest of February and well into March. When spring began to announce its arrival, we knew we could not leave the poisoned carcass because spring arrivals such as eagles and bears would doubtless scavenge what they could.

With two snowmobiles, towropes, needle bars, and axes, we set off to try and pry the horse loose from the ice. We chiseled and chopped, levered and pulled, but all to no avail. When we gave the cadaver a solid whack to the ribs with the back of the axe, the resonance was loud and clear; the wolves had created their very own version of a bass drum. To resolve the situation, we had to cut the horse in two before we could move it out from the creek. From there, it was merely a question of hauling it to the nearest disposal facility.

Yes, it was a sad and untimely end for the horse, but it made us wonder who had been the first to chase animals off cliffs. Did the aboriginals learn from watching the wolves, or could it have been the other way round?

The horse owner was advised of our efforts and the subsequent results. He was not really very impressed, but at least he concurred the wolves had not shown up again that winter. For that, he was grateful.

EPILOGUE.

As you have read, my career in Fish and Wildlife was an adventure. When I started out on this project, I simply had a mind to leave some of these stories for my grandchildren. Like any grandparent, I want them to live life to the fullest just as I did! However, I was persuaded that others too would enjoy my experiences almost as much as me, which is why this book came into being. As it took shape, it dawned on me very quickly that I had too many stories for the one book, there would have to be at least two. So if you enjoyed reading this one, keep your eyes open for the next one! So many of these experiences were just too much fun to keep to myself, I had to share them with somebody!

There are plenty more.

For additional copies of Poachers, Cranberries and Snowshoes, please contact your local book store or the publisher. To arrange author interviews, special events or book signings contact:

JBS Publishing
Rural Route 3
Rocky Mountain House A.B.
T4T 2A3
email: cesj1 @ telus.net
Phone 403 845 4234